Y0-AGU-959

PRAISE FOR *BETTER ALLIES*

"I tore through *Better Allies*, and you will too. Karen Catlin has brought clarity to the challenges underrepresented people face at work. Read this book if you want advice on how to be a better ally, on how to create a more inclusive culture, and on how to increase your competitive advantage around hiring and retaining talent." **—Norm Meyrowitz**
former President of Products, Macromedia

"Calling all allies! Here is your one-stop manual for becoming better as an advocate, champion, and ally for marginalized colleagues in the workplace. Catlin's rich experience as an executive in the tech world infuses each of her immensely practical allyship strategies with deep wisdom from the trenches. This amazing book is both an invitation and a roadmap to every person and organization committed to making the workplace fully inclusive."
—Brad Johnson, PhD and **David G. Smith, PhD**
authors of *Athena Rising: How and Why Men Should Mentor Women*

"Some people have it harder than you at work. This is just true. Get over it. And, yes, there are many permutations of this dynamic involving class, color, race, sexual orientation and a few thousand other ways people are different from each other. We tend to not notice it, or not do anything about it, at least partly because we're not sure what to do. Fortunately, we now have *Better Allies*. It's incredibly complete and packed with practical advice to help you start to make a difference in your organization." **—Joe Dunn**
Executive Coach and Radical Candor Guru

"As a global business strategist with a plural board career, I am passionate regarding how imperative it is in today's world that companies must sharpen their competitive advantage by attracting and retaining top talent. *Better Allies* is a thoughtful and insightful book, offering a tool kit of meaningful, actionable ideas for the reader of how to create a meaningful and engaging workplace." **—Eugenia Ulasewicz**
former President, Burberry America

"Navigating today's business landscape requires everyone to build their ability to support colleagues and coach others. This book will give you valuable insights and practical advice on being a better ally. It's an eye-opening, powerful approach." **—Tom Hale**
President, SurveyMonkey

"Karen Catlin has created an accessible, practical everyday guide to becoming a better ally. Whether you are just starting out or you've been an ally for years, everyone can learn something new from this terrific book." **—Elizabeth Ames**
Leadership Committee of Time's Up Tech
and Founder, Allies Together

"*Better Allies* is an important book for outcome-focused executives, however we classify ourselves. As someone who mentors a broad set of up-and-coming product managers and product leaders, I see every day how urgently we need to widen our lenses to spot emerging talent we've often overlooked—even as so many product leadership roles remain unfilled. Karen Catlin provides a range of actionable, motivating, effective tools for growing more diverse teams so that we can deliver more successful products. *Better Allies* can help each of us be better allies." **—Rich Mironov**
startup CEO and author of *The Art of Product Management*

"Ever found yourself wondering 'How can I better support diversity and inclusion in the workplace?' In *Better Allies*, Karen Catlin breaks it down and helps to guide the conversation. This book is just the beginning of a grassroots movement. And it's going to help make a big difference to workplaces everywhere." **—Brad Arkin**
Vice President and Chief Security Officer, Adobe

"As businesses continue to focus on local and global expansion, I believe success lies in seeking and embracing differing cultural perspectives. The first step is to have a workforce which is reflective of their target customer. By including and advocating for people of all genders, cultures and lifestyles, and ensuring they are reflected in all levels of the company from the board room to the mail room, businesses will develop a practice of empathy and understanding which will translate into more meaningful connections, thus products and services people believe in. Better Allies paves a road to this success." **—Steve Johnson**
Vice President of Experience Design and Innovation, Netflix

"As men, we have a whole lot of privilege. And we can use that privilege to open doors and bring more diversity into 'the room where it happens.' In *Better Allies*, you'll learn practical steps to do exactly that and create a more inclusive workplace. Be a better man and read this book now." **—Ray Arata**
Co-Founder Inclusionary Leadership Group

Better Allies

Everyday Actions to Create
Inclusive, Engaging
Workplaces

KAREN CATLIN

Better Allies Press

BETTER ALLIES: Everyday Actions to Create Inclusive, Engaging Workplaces. Copyright © 2019 by Karen Catlin. Printed in the United States of America.

Published by Better Allies Press.
www.betterallies.com

All rights reserved. No part of this book may be used or reproduced in any manner whatsoever without written permission of the Publisher, except for the inclusion of brief quotations in a review. For permission to quote or for bulk orders, please contact info@betterallies.com.

FIRST EDITION

Hardcover ISBN: 978-1-7327233-1-3
Softcover ISBN: 978-1-7327233-0-6
eBook ISBN: 978-1-7327233-2-0

Editing: Sally McGraw
Cover design: Laura Duffy
Copyediting: Alex Kapitan

www.karencatlin.com

CONTENTS

INTRODUCTION

A diverse and inclusive workplace has a certain buzz about it. Employees are thriving, and they love their work. Engagement survey scores are through the roof. People from different backgrounds, ethnicities, genders, sexual orientations, ages, and abilities are hired and set up for success—and they want their friends to work there too, because it's so awesome.

Unfortunately, diverse and inclusive workplaces are elusive. They are both difficult to find and hard to create. Here we are, in the twenty-first century, reading headline after headline about discrimination in professional settings: "60% of Women in Silicon Valley Have Been Sexually Harassed" (*Fast Company*, 2016), "Why Doesn't Silicon Valley Hire Black Coders?" (*Bloomberg*, 2016), "Mass Firings at Uber as Sexual Harassment Scandal Grows" (*Vanity Fair*, 2017), "Tech Leavers Study: Tech is a hostile work environment if you're not a straight white dude" (*Jax Enter*, 2017), "Silicon Valley Investor Resigns after Harassment Claims: 'I'm a Creep. I'm

Sorry.'" (CNN, 2017), "Google Engineer's Anti-diversity Manifesto Sparks Outrage" (CNET, 2017), "Big Tech, Little Diversity: Blacks Comprise 3% of Silicon Valley Talent" (*Industry Week*, 2018), and "Report Shows Diversity in Tech Has Only Gotten Worse" (KPIX San Francisco, 2018).

The strides that have been made in workforce equity and diversity are significant, but there are still miles to go. The evidence of bias and oppression is both codified and anecdotal. Research has revealed the extent of the barriers faced by women, people of color, LGBTQ people, people with disabilities, and members of other underrepresented groups in the workplace—from being consistently under-hired, overlooked, and excluded from professional opportunities to being subjected to harassment and abuse on the job.

At the same time, there's growing awareness about the importance of diversity in the workforce. A movement is building, encouraging unbiased hiring practices and lauding the strengths of varied labor pools. Leaders who prioritize equity in hiring often influence their peers, creating a ripple effect of inclusion. As well they should, because the benefits are clear: Study after study shows that diverse teams create more innovative solutions, they're more adept at solving difficult problems, and they achieve better financial success.[1]

Yet this is not common knowledge. What's more, people in positions of privilege are often unaware of issues facing underrepresented groups working in their industry.

My own observations about these worrying trends come from twenty-five years of working in the tech industry. I first noticed the problem when I was working as a vice president of engineering at Adobe. While I was keenly aware that women had little chance of breaking into senior leadership roles, many of my male colleagues were oblivious. They firmly believed Adobe was a meritocracy. They told me it was the kind of company where men and women had an equal chance of getting ahead and clung to this belief even though our demographics proved otherwise. Men dominated the senior leadership roles across the organization, and although according to my calculations at the time, women made up a third of the company's directors and senior directors, that number dropped to just 18 percent at the vice president level.

I began to see discrimination bubbling up in overt and covert ways. I remember talking with a man on my staff who needed to fill a senior role on his team. When I asked if he planned to promote his top employee into the role, he replied that she had young children at home and he felt sure that she wouldn't want all the travel that would come with the promotion. I countered, saying that this was her decision to make, not his. (He decided to make her the offer, which she accepted. She went on to totally rock the role.)

And then there was the 2014 Grace Hopper Celebration of Women in Computing, a troubling moment for gender diversity in tech. At the event, Satya Nadella, the newly appointed CEO of Microsoft, proclaimed that women shouldn't ask for raises. Instead, he suggested that they should have faith and wait for the system to give them the pay rates they deserved.[2] This advice was perplexing to women in the audience who worked in an industry where they earned between 4 percent and 45 percent less than men in the same roles.[3] Despite being constantly overlooked and underpaid, the advice they were being given was to sit on their hands? They charged back on social media, and Satya soon apologized.

But that wasn't all. The conference also featured a male allies panel. Male leaders from Facebook, Google, Intuit, and GoDaddy shared what they had done to improve gender diversity within their prominent companies. Unfortunately, the panel missed its mark. The speakers were clueless about the challenges their female employees faced, reiterating tired platitudes about how hard work pays off and how confidence is a huge asset to working women.[4] It was a disaster, and one that enraged people of all genders.

As the years rolled by, more and more appalling stats about the hiring and promotion of people of color in my industry surfaced. A 2017 report by the Ascend Foundation included data from hundreds of Silicon Valley companies, including Apple, Cisco, Facebook, Google, HP, Intel, Twitter, and Yelp, and showed that race is an increasingly more significant impediment than gender to climbing the management ladder.[5] That same year, Recode reported that Black and Latinx[i] employees held only 4 percent to 10 percent of leadership roles at seven major tech companies.[6] This all came to light in the wake of tech companies prioritizing growth over everything else, even when it enabled discrimination. For example, Nextdoor users are notorious for posting racist "crime and safety" alerts targeting their neighbors of color, and Airbnb found that "guests with 'distinctively African American names' are 16% less likely to be accepted than identical guests with white-sounding names."[7] It seemed that the tech industry was unaware of its ingrained racist tendencies in both internal policies and consumer-facing product-building practices.

Reports of workplace sexism, racism, and other discrimination are rampant across nearly all industries. These reports are remarkably varied. Some are blatant examples of gender-based harassment or racial bias. Others are more

---

[i] *Latinx* is a gender-neutral term that replaces *Latino* and *Latina/o* in order to refer inclusively to all people of Latin American descent or culture.

subtle, such as homophobic jokes in work-only chats, promotional giveaways ordered only in men's sizes, people of color hearing rude comments about their hair, or female partners not being invited on a guys-only coworker outing.

While there's no denying that there's much work left to do, it's not all doom and gloom. Throughout this book, you'll find dozens of stories that show the flip side of this trend, illustrating how allies have made a lasting difference at their companies. My hope is that many more allies will be inspired to take action in the future, and that my inbox will be inundated with success stories.

Why I care

When releasing workforce demographic data, companies often include quotes from white, straight, able-bodied male leaders about the importance of diversity. These men truly believe they're creating meritocracies, that they're treating women and people from other underrepresented groups equitably. Their hearts seem to be in the right place. However, when I look dispassionately at the stories they tell and their lack of meaningful actions to actually diversify their workforces, it becomes clear that many of these leaders are *not* doing everything they can. They're missing opportunities to be authentic allies.

But here's the real kicker: they're also missing out on gaining a competitive advantage. By creating cultures where all people can do their best work and thrive, active allies build businesses that attract the best and brightest talent. The cream of the crop wants to work with and for them, which sounds ideal, yet so few companies commit to diversity in meaningful and lasting ways. So few hit the mark. So few allies make real change possible.

Is it really that hard to act as an ally for underrepresented people in a workplace?

I didn't think so, and after years of observation, I decided to take action. I wanted to learn what meaningful allyship for underrepresented groups in tech might look like. To play what I hoped was at least a small role in making my own industry more diverse and inclusive. To help create workplaces where my friends, my coaching clients, and my daughter (who has wanted to be a software engineer since she was little) could do their best work and thrive.

So in 2014, I started tweeting from an anonymous handle, @betterallies, with the goal of sharing straightforward, simple actions that anyone could take to make their workplace more inclusive. I wanted to demystify allyship and help people in positions of power—particularly men—do their part. I wanted to draw attention to the problem but also offer actionable solutions. Through my tweeting, coupled with responses to my posts and interactions with others working in tech, I've amassed many great examples of how allies do act, or should act, in real workplace scenarios. And because they're far too good to let them fade into the Twitter twilight, I'm sharing them in this book.

This is a guide to help you spot situations in which you can be a better ally, not just to women but to all marginalized groups. If you've got the will to support your underrepresented colleagues, you're already ahead of the pack. I'll give you actionable tips so you can transform that will into meaningful change. While my primary audience is men in the workplace, this book can be helpful to anyone who is in a position of power. It just so happens that, in our current economic climate, men hold most of these positions.

As I wrote each chapter, I did my best to discuss the challenges facing all marginalized groups, with a particular focus on women, people of color, people with disabilities, and LGBTQ people. That said, my own experience as a white, straight, cisgender,[ii] able-bodied woman in tech means that gender inequality is my entry point and greatest area of expertise. My personal experience is bound to influence my perspective, but I've done my best to highlight research and stories that reflect the experiences of other groups in other industries and model what it's like to be an ally to all marginalized groups.

Although it's designed to be read cover to cover, I hope you'll also refer to this book when you want to level up your ally skills and sharpen your competitive advantage around attracting and retaining talent. Use it as a resource when you need to help others course correct during the hiring process, in meetings, at events, or during performance review time. I'd love to see this book on desks everywhere, serving as an accessible and supportive resource for aspiring allies and the underrepresented people they work with and for.

Being an ally is a journey, and it's a journey that I myself am still on. I'm thrilled that you'll be joining me.

[ii] *Cisgender* is a relatively new word that means a person is not transgender; that one's gender identity (or internal sense of self) aligns, according to societal expectations, with the sex assigned at birth.

PART ONE

WATCHING AND OBSERVING AS AN ALLY

1

THE ALLY JOURNEY

Allyship is a process. Even seasoned allies with wide open minds are constantly learning and absorbing new information about how to leverage their privilege to support people who are different from them. We all have perspectives that are shaped by our own experiences, so we can't possibly imagine or understand all of the other viewpoints that exist in the world. We must learn about them as we encounter them, and adjust our mindsets accordingly. So your first tip for being an ally is to be open to learning, improving, and changing your opinion. And recognize that being an ally is a journey.

This may seem frustrating at first, because it's tempting to want to earn an ally badge and consider oneself to be a lifetime member of the Genuinely Good Human Beings Club. I get it. If this sounds like you, I wrote this book to help you move forward, and I guarantee you'll pick up actionable ideas to be a better ally.

Instead of feeling frustrated that you'll never reach some mythical, fully fledged ally status, remember that we're all learning together. The ally journey is an enlightening and worthwhile one, even though it's a perpetually ongoing one. And people with privilege who are *truly* dedicated to the empowerment of all embrace the fact that doing so means being in a constant state of learning.

Speaking of which, the time has come to discuss privilege in both abstract and concrete terms. I promise to keep it nonjudgmental and encouragement focused!

Let's talk about the "p-word"

Understanding privilege is key to becoming a better ally. At its core, privilege is a set of unearned benefits given to people who fit into a specific social group. Due to our race, class, gender, sexual orientation, language, geographical location, ability, religion, and more, all of us have greater or lesser access to resources and social power.

People who are marginalized in multiple ways experience amplified marginalization and drastically reduced privilege. This is due to intersectionality, the fact that the intersection of someone's identities creates an intersection of overlapping and compounded oppressions.[8] I appreciate this example by Kittu Pannu, who wrote about intersectionality in the LGBT community for Impakter:

> *One could assume that a black, queer woman would, in essence, have a more difficult life experience than a heterosexual white male just by virtue of her experiences as a woman, compounded with her experience as a black person, and topping it off with her queer identity. Her life will be just a little harsher, her earning potential just short of the people around her, her ability to say with certainty that she gets everything she deserves not as strong as a white male's ability. She would have to work that much harder to be taken seriously in today's heteronormative, white, male-dominated world.[9]*

The term *intersectionality* was originally coined by Kimberlé Crenshaw in her 1989 essay "Mapping the Margins: Intersectionality, Identity Politics, and Violence against Women of Color," and she explores it further in her excellent TED talk, "The Urgency of Intersectionality."[10] In nearly all cases, being marginalized in multiple ways leads to diminished privilege and increased risk of discrimination and violence.

Now, here's where it gets tricky: Privilege is often invisible to those who have it. This means that many people get defensive when someone points out their privilege. It's tempting to think of privilege as being associated with extreme unearned advantages like having a massive family trust fund or being related to some influential person. Having one's privilege pointed out might feel like the equivalent of being told that one is lazy, lucky, or undeserving of good things—or that one's life has been easy. Many people are quick to respond that they've had their fair share of difficulties and faced down prejudices, too.

But doing this means forgetting that privilege is simply a system of advantages granted to all people in a given group. It's a social structure that has become endemic to human cultures. It's not about who you are as an individual as much as it is about which groups you belong to, and how those groups are viewed and treated by society. A person isn't privileged because of being a rotten, freeloading bum, they're privileged because they're white or middle-class or cisgender.

Being privileged doesn't mean you've never worked hard, and it doesn't necessarily mean that your life has been easy. Here's a fabulous analogy from Sian Ferguson via the website Everyday Feminism:

> *Let's say both you and your friend decide to go cycling. You decide to cycle for the same distance, but you take different routes. You take a route that is a bit bumpy. More often than*

not, you go down roads that are at a slight decline. It's very hot, but the wind is at [sic] usually at your back. You eventually get to your destination, but you're sunburnt, your legs are aching, you're out of breath, and you have a cramp.

When you eventually meet up with your friend, she says that the ride was awful for her. It was also bumpy. The road she took was at an incline the entire time. She was even more sunburnt than you because she had no sunscreen. At one point, a strong gust of wind blew her over and she hurt her foot. She ran out of water halfway through. When she hears about your route, she remarks that your experience seemed easier than hers.

Does that mean that you didn't cycle to the best of your ability? Does it mean that you didn't face obstacles? Does it mean that you didn't work hard? No. What it means is that you didn't face the obstacles she faced.

Privilege doesn't mean your life is easy or that you didn't work hard. It simply means that you don't have to face the obstacles others have to endure. It means that life is more difficult for those who don't have the systemic privilege you have.[11]

Look at any business segment, and you'll find people who have more privilege than others. In today's tech industry, they tend to be straight white men. Perhaps they attended highly selective universities such as Stanford, MIT, or an Ivy League school. They may have strong networks of people in similar positions of privilege. They are the majority.

Yet privilege is not limited to straight white guys.

I'm fortunate to have a lot of privilege. I'm white, straight, able-bodied, and a U.S. citizen. I hold a degree in computer science from an Ivy League school. I'm a published author and a TEDx speaker. Formerly, I was a vice president of engineering at a well-known tech company. Yup. That's a lot of privilege. And my experience is a great reminder that people who are members of systematically oppressed groups (such as women) can still have privilege due to their membership in other groups (such as being white, straight, etc.).

Fifty potential privileges in the workplace

Now for the hard part: Take a moment to examine your own privilege, and reflect on the benefits or obstacles you face at work. Using the list below, quiz yourself by measuring how your privilege compares to your coworkers.

As you review this list, keep a tally. Note any items that surprise you and make you wonder, "Does anyone actually face this challenge?"

1. You are white.
2. You are male.
3. You are straight.
4. You are cisgender (you identify as the gender you were assigned at birth).
5. You're not significantly younger or older than your coworkers.
6. You don't have any disabilities, visible or otherwise.
7. You have a college degree.
8. You attended an elite university.
9. You were born in the United States or you're a citizen of the United States.
10. English is your first language.
11. You don't receive comments about your accent or the way you pronounce certain words.
12. You've never been passed over for a job (or fired from one) based on your gender, race or ethnicity, religion, age, body shape or size, disability, or sexual orientation.
13. You are partnered and feel comfortable speaking openly about your significant other.

14. You're not the primary caregiver for anyone else.
15. You feel welcome at networking opportunities.
16. You aren't asked to do menial tasks that colleagues of another gender or race are asked to do.
17. Others don't routinely assume you're a lower seniority level than you are.
18. You feel comfortable actively and effectively contributing to meetings you attend.
19. You're rarely interrupted or ignored in meetings.
20. You are confident that if you raise an idea in a meeting, you'll be credited for that idea.
21. Your manager maintains eye contact when speaking to you.
22. You recently received feedback about a technical skill you need to learn.
23. You have spare time to spend on open source projects or learning new technologies.
24. You haven't been told to wait your turn for a promotion or plum project assignment behind an equally qualified peer.
25. You have gotten a job or a promotion with the help of a social, family, or school-related connection.
26. You can talk about politically or identity-oriented extracurricular activities without fear of judgment or bias from colleagues.
27. You can observe the holy days in your religious tradition without having to use vacation days.
28. You feel welcome and valued on group projects.
29. You've never been called a "diversity hire."
30. When meeting people at technical events, they assume you're attending in a technical role (versus being the partner of an attendee or that you work in a non-technical role).
31. At events, people don't mistake you for a member of the catering staff.
32. You don't receive unwanted sexual advances at work.

33. You haven't had to change teams or companies because of harassment.
34. You feel physically safe at work and at professional events.
35. You feel safe leaving work late at night and going home after evening events.
36. You have stable housing.
37. You're confident that if you were to lose your job, you'd be able to land another one without worrying about paying bills.
38. You can afford to join out-of-office lunches or after-work social activities.
39. You can manage monthly payments on any debt you have.
40. You never have to decide which bills to pay or go without meals because of not being able to afford food.
41. You're not financially supporting a parent, grandparent, sibling, or other extended family member(s).
42. You have a partner who takes on a large share of household and family responsibilities.
43. You're rarely, if ever, late to work or miss work because of a child's illness or family emergency.
44. You don't have a long career gap on your resume.
45. You've never been arrested, incarcerated, or charged with a criminal offense.
46. People never touch you or your hair without consent.
47. You're comfortable speaking in meetings, without worrying someone will find a flaw in your logic and prove you're not qualified to be there.
48. You don't receive abusive comments on social media.
49. You don't remember the last time someone was condescending or overly pedantic when explaining a topic to you.
50. You don't depend on a sponsor, mentor, or any other ally to be respected and taken seriously.

Even if you happen to have all fifty of the above privileges, the intent here is not to make you feel guilty or ashamed. By contrast, the invitation is simply to be aware of your advantages and leverage them empathetically; beating yourself up about them is totally counterproductive.

That said, privilege is often a key ingredient in cultivating professional confidence: Confidence that you can leverage your network to get a new job, raise capital for a start-up, find a publisher for your book, or score a speaking engagement. Confidence that when you make a killer point at the meeting, others will pay attention. Confidence that people will direct questions to you if you're the expert in the room. Confidence that you're getting paid equitably. Confidence that other attendees at a networking social event will assume you're qualified to be there, and not part of the waitstaff. Confidence that people believe you landed your current role because of experience and potential, not solely because you're a woman or a person of color. The list goes on.

Because of my privilege, I know I've received many benefits over my career, and those benefits have empowered me with confidence. I feel ready to use my standing to help foster confidence in others now, and if you are also in a position to do so, I hope you'll join me.

Roles allies can play

It's up to people who hold positions of privilege to be active allies to those with less access, and take responsibility for making changes that will help others be successful. Active allies utilize their credibility to create a more inclusive workplace where everyone can thrive, and they find ways to make their privilege work for others.

And wielding privilege as an ally doesn't have to be hard. I've seen allies at all levels take action with simple, everyday efforts that made a difference. Often a big difference! Here are a few roles that allies can choose to play to support colleagues from underrepresented groups in beneficial ways.[12]

THE SPONSOR

I once worked for a software company that was acquired by a larger company. In the first few months following the acquisition, I noticed something interesting. My new manager, Digby Horner—who had been at the larger company for many years—said things in meetings along the lines of: "What I learned from Karen is the following ..."

By doing this, Digby helped me build credibility with my new colleagues. He took action as an ally, using his position of privilege to sponsor me. His shout-outs made a difference, and definitely made me feel great.

When an ally takes on the role of the Sponsor, they vocally support the work of colleagues from underrepresented groups in all contexts, but specifically in situations that will help boost those colleagues' standing and reputations.

Other ways to act as a Sponsor:

- Talk about the expertise you see in others, especially during performance calibrations and promotion discussions.
- Recommend people for stretch assignments and learning opportunities.
- Share colleagues' career goals with influencers.

THE CHAMPION

In May 2015, Andrew Grill was a Global Managing Partner at IBM and a speaker at the Online Influence Conference. He was on a panel along with five other men when a female member of the audience posed the obvious question to the all-male lineup: "Where are the women?"

The moderator then asked the panelists to address the topic of gender diversity, and Andrew, after sharing some of his thoughts, quickly realized he wasn't the best person to respond. In fact, none of the panelists were. He instead asked the woman who asked the question, Miranda Bishop, to take his place on the panel. By stepping aside, Andrew made a bold statement in support of gender diversity on stage and championed Miranda at the same time.[13]

Since then, the nonprofit organization GenderAvenger has created a pledge to reduce the frequency all-male panels at conferences and events. It reads, "I will not serve as a panelist at a public conference when there are no women on the panel." Anyone can sign the pledge on their website, genderavenger.com.

When an ally takes on the role of the Champion, that ally acts similarly to the Sponsor, but does so in more public venues. Champions willingly defer to colleagues from under-represented groups in meetings and in visible, industry-wide events and conferences, sending meaningful messages to large audiences.

Other ways to act as a Champion:

- Direct questions about specific or technical topics to employees with subject-matter expertise instead of answering them yourself.
- Advocate for more women, people of color, and members of other underrepresented groups as keynote speakers and panelists.
- If you are asked to keynote or serve in a similar public role and know someone from an underrepresented group who'd be an equally good fit (or better), recommend that person (after asking them first if they'd like to be put forward).

THE AMPLIFIER

In a Slack channel for female technical leaders, I met a data engineer who was working at a sixty-person start-up. One team inside the company had an unproductive meeting culture that was starting to feel truly toxic. Yelling and interrupting frequently took place at the team's meetings, and women, in particular, felt they couldn't voice their opinions without being shouted over.

One of this engineer's colleagues decided to take action to ensure that the voices of those who weren't shouting would be heard. She introduced communication guidelines for a weekly meeting, and saw an immediate improvement. The guidelines included assigning a meeting mediator (team members would take turns in this role), setting clear objectives and an agenda for every meeting, conducting a meeting evaluation by every participant at the end of every meeting, and reminding the members to be respectful and practice active listening.

When an ally takes on the role of the Amplifier, that ally works to ensure that marginalized voices are both heard and respected. This type of allyship can take many forms, but is focused on representation within communication.

Other ways to act as an Amplifier:

- When someone proposes a good idea, repeat it and give them credit. For example: "I agree with Helen's recommendation for improving our net promoter score."
- Create a code of conduct for meetings and any shared communication medium including email, chat, Slack, and so forth.
- Invite members of underrepresented groups within your company to speak at staff meetings, write for company-wide newsletters, or take on other highly visible roles.

THE ADVOCATE

Shortly after she became CEO of YouTube, Susan Wojcicki spoke up about how tech industry titan Bill Campbell had advocated for her. In an article for *Vanity Fair*, she wrote:

> *I learned about an important invitation-only conference convening most of the top leaders in tech and media, yet my name was left off the guest list. Many of the invitees were my*

peers, meaning that YouTube wouldn't be represented while deals were cut and plans were made. I started to question whether I even belonged at the conference. But rather than let it go, I turned to Bill, someone I knew had a lot of influence and could help fix the situation. He immediately recognized I had a rightful place at the event and within a day he worked his magic and I received my invitation.[14]

When an ally takes on the role of the Advocate, that ally uses their power and influence to bring peers from underrepresented groups into highly exclusive circles. The Advocate recognizes and addresses unjust omissions, holding their peers accountable for including qualified colleagues of all genders, races and ethnicities, abilities, ages, body shapes and sizes, religions, and sexual orientations.

Other ways to act as an Advocate:

- Look closely at the invite list for events, strategic planning meetings, dinners with key partners, and other career-building opportunities. If you see someone from a marginalized group missing, advocate for them to be invited.

- Offer to introduce colleagues from underrepresented groups to influential people in your network.

- Ask someone from an underrepresented group to be a coauthor or collaborator on a proposal or conference submission.

THE SCHOLAR

I'm a member of the Women's CLUB of Silicon Valley, a nonprofit leadership incubator for women. Many of our events are open to guests, who come to hear the speakers and participate in our workshops. Most guests are women, so it stood out when a male guest started attending our events. I asked one of my friends who he was, and she told me he was a former colleague who wanted to better understand the challenges women face in the workplace. He spent many evenings at our events, listening and absorbing information about the issues we discussed so he could be a better ally.

When an ally takes on the role of the Scholar, that ally seeks to learn as much as possible about the challenges and prejudices faced by colleagues from marginalized groups. It's important to note that Scholars never insert their own opinions, experiences, or ideas, but instead simply listen and learn. They also don't expect marginalized people to provide links to research proving that bias exists or to summaries of best practices. Scholars do their own research to seek out the relevant information.

Other ways to act as a Scholar:

- Investigate and read publications, podcasts, or social media by and about underrepresented groups within your industry.
- Ask coworkers from marginalized groups about their experience working at your company.
- If your company or industry has specific discussion groups or Slack channels for members of

underrepresented groups, ask if they'd be comfortable letting you sit in to observe. Asking is essential: Your presence may cause members to censor themselves, so be sure to check in before showing up.

THE UPSTANDER

I remember being impressed by Lisa, a white software engineer who stepped outside of her comfort zone to be an ally. When asked to name her "spirit animal" as part of a team-building exercise, Lisa spoke up. She wasn't comfortable taking part in an exercise that appropriated Native American spiritual traditions.

When an ally takes on the role of the Upstander, that ally acts as the *opposite* of a bystander. The Upstander is someone who sees wrongdoing and acts to combat it. This person pushes back on offensive comments or jokes, even if no one within earshot might be offended or hurt.

Other ways to act as an Upstander:

- Always speak up if you witness behavior or speech that is degrading or offensive. Explain your stance so everyone is clear about why you are raising the issue.
- In meetings, shut down off-topic questions that are asked only to test the presenter.
- Take action if you see anyone in your company being bullied or harassed. Simply insert yourself into a conversation with a comment like, "Hi! What are you folks discussing?" and then check in with the victim

privately. Ask if they are okay and if they want you to say something.

THE CONFIDANT

A couple of years ago, I spoke with Emily, a college-aged intern who told me about a one-on-one meeting with her mentor. When he asked what she wanted to do post-graduation, Emily emphasized that her top priority was to find an inclusive work environment. When he asked why, she shared her experience working at a previous internship. Her manager there wouldn't make eye contact with her, and he directed all technical questions about her project to her coding partner, a male intern. The mentor listened to Emily, incredulous at first but quickly believing her. Although he had heard rumors, before she shared this experience with him he hadn't truly believed things like this happened. By listening and believing, he both supported his mentee and validated her experience in the tech industry.

When an ally takes on the role of the Confidant, that ally creates a safe space for members of underrepresented groups to express their fears, frustrations, and needs. Simply listening to their stories and trusting that they're being truthful creates a protective layer of support.

Other ways to act as a Confidant:

- Believe others' experiences. Don't assume something couldn't happen just because you haven't personally experienced it.

- Listen and ask questions when someone describes an experience you haven't had. Don't jump in with your personal stories.
- If you are a manager, hold regular "office hours" and encourage all of your team members to speak with you about issues that are troubling them.

The perfectly imperfect ally

In this chapter, I've shared just a few examples of how people with privilege have acted as allies in specific roles. It's important to note that, while these people all chose to use their power to support others, they're humans and therefore not perfect. And they don't need to be. The best allies are willing to make mistakes and keep trying. They acknowledge when they're wrong or could do better, and correct their course. They resist getting defensive and insisting that they're already doing enough. They listen and learn. They iterate.

And there are many opportunities in every workplace to listen, learn, and take action as allies. It's something anyone can do. In the coming chapters, we'll explore how to spot situations where you can be a better ally, and everyday actions that will make a difference.

Actions for Better Allies:
Understand Your Privilege and Use It for Good

An important part of allyship is being open to learning, improving, and taking action.

- Review the list of fifty potential privileges in the workplace that was included in this chapter. How many apply to you?

- Identify at least one way you can be a better ally, using the archetypes in this chapter.

- Understand that being an ally is a journey. We all make mistakes. Don't let that hold you back from taking action.

2

KNIGHTS VERSUS ALLIES

In June 2017, I published an article on Opensource.com about why I started Better Allies.[15] Given the website's large reader base and boatload of followers on Twitter, I knew it would help increase awareness of my initiative. I also had a feeling it might generate some criticism. As Jason van Gumster wrote previously to the open source community, "Haters are an inevitable part of sharing your work."[16]

So on publication day, I mentally prepared myself; hoping for support, yet ready to handle any backlash. When I checked Twitter early in the morning, I saw lots of great comments and retweets of the article. Phew!

Next came responses from some folks who disagreed, saying things like, "I'm here to earn my paycheck, not take care of other people." (Expletives removed. Several of these folks needed to both vent *and* swear.) And there were a handful of pointed jabs calling me a creep and instructing me to eff off. Nothing I couldn't handle.

But then ... a surprise. I saw a few critical tweets that made me think deeply about my work on Better Allies and how it might be perceived. These tweets were from women who completely dismissed the need for allies. Women who didn't want to be placed in a homogeneous group that couldn't speak for themselves. Women who bristled at the implied need for knights to ride in on white horses and save them from toxic workplace cultures.

I'd expected to hear from some haters, but to learn from them? That caught me off guard.

It also got me thinking about how actions that were meant to be supportive could feel patronizing. I realized that good intentions were never going to be enough. Real allies needed to carefully consider the repercussions of their actions, too. These tweets also helped me refine my own goals: I don't want to be a knight riding in to save the day. I don't want to view underrepresented folks as virtual damsels in distress. I don't want to serve as anyone's protector. No. Never. Instead, I want to transform current workplace cultures into ones where everyone can thrive. I want to question the norms that have allowed folks like me to get ahead, encourage productive conversation around prejudices, and take everyday actions to support members of marginalized groups. And I want to bring others along on this journey.

I know now that part of that journey will involve teaching myself and others how to translate our heartfelt intentions into meaningful, constructive actions—and avoid being inadvertently condescending or patronizing.

How to tell a knight from an ally

So, what is the difference between ally actions and knight actions? I believe it comes down to whether they ultimately create systemic change or not. Here are some examples:

Scenario 1

Imagine you are part of a hiring committee, and you realize the group is measuring candidates inconsistently. Group members are using subjective criteria that treat the one candidate from an underrepresented group less favorably than the rest of the pool. Let's call that candidate Willie.

The group's biased objections to Willie might sound like, "I just didn't click with him. I can't quite put my finger on it." Or, "I don't think I'd feel comfortable putting him in front of customers." Or perhaps someone might say, "Willie doesn't have the four to six years of coding experience listed in the job description," even though other candidates who also lacked that experience were given a thumbs-up.

A knight would push back to give Willie a better chance, trying to save him from being eliminated from the hiring process. The knight might say, "I think Willie can do the job. In fact, I'll personally mentor him to help him be successful." This might result in a positive outcome for one marginalized person, but it is less likely to have a lasting impact on hiring policies.

By contrast, an ally would push back on this specific decision *and* seek systemic change so that the situation would not occur again. For example, the ally might say, "Folks, let's step back. I'm concerned we're not consistently evaluating our candidates. Let's identify objective criteria that we can use to measure everyone. Moving forward, I'd like to discuss how we can make this a best practice for all hiring committees."

Scenario 2

Imagine noticing a person from an underrepresented group being interrupted in a meeting. Let's call her Mia. She's tried to make her point a few times, but someone always cuts her off.

A knight might step in to save her by saying, "I think Mia was making a good point. Let me summarize." If the knight has substantially more privilege than Mia, it might feel appropriate to both acknowledge her idea and put it into their own words. After all, that would mean using their power to highlight her talent. However, it might also result in listeners remembering the knight's recap more clearly than Mia's initial explanation, and crediting the knight with the idea.

An ally would redirect the conversation back to Mia's capable hands with, "I'd like to get back to what Mia was saying." An ally would do this consistently, any time they witnessed someone being talked over. The ally could also institute a no-interruption rule for future meetings or an overall code of conduct that creates a respectful environment for all speakers. (More on this in Chapter 5.)

Scenario 3

I recently coached a client, Amanda, who led a large department of highly skilled tech workers. While working on performance rankings, she noticed that one woman's salary was significantly lower than that of her male peers.

Acting as a knight would have been the easiest route for Amanda to take. With one quick update to a spreadsheet, she could have adjusted that employee's salary. She could have fixed the inequity and felt good about treating that woman more fairly. But Amanda recognized that she could use her position and privilege to do more, to push beyond helping just one person.

Instead, Amanda led an initiative to perform a salary review by gender, not just for her department but for her company as a whole. It was a lot more work, but it led to changes that supported the entire employee base. She also ensured that the compensation processes would treat new hires and existing employees fairly and equitably; it created lasting, systemic change.

Amanda's initiative even uncovered some unexpected data: In addition to identifying women who were underpaid, she found a handful of men whose salaries were significantly lower than the salaries of their peers. Because her goal was to treat everyone equitably and not just identify women who were underpaid, she recommended compensation audits for the departments where those discrepancies were found. Now that's what I call allyship.

Scenario 4

Across the tech industry, there are many leaders who act as Sponsors, Champions, and Advocates. They recommend individuals for stretch assignments. They talk about others' accomplishments to highlight the impact they're making on the business. They use their organizational clout to open doors.

Sheree Atcheson, Tech Respect & Inclusion Manager at Deloitte, told me about her sponsor and how he helps her to grow her career. He actively opts out of opportunities, passing them along to her instead. He mentions her in meetings and ensures that clients have her contact info so they can follow up with her directly. In her words, "He enables me to create stronger business connections."

When Sheree told me about her sponsor, I initially thought, "What a good guy." But I also wondered if he was truly an ally or more of a knight, setting her up for success to "save" her from being stuck at a certain level of her career.

Sheree quickly disagreed. She told me that he also works to change the culture so that other leaders are acting as sponsors, passing along opportunities. Plus, she pointed out that he actively gives her constructive feedback, helping her to grow and be less dependent on him to open career doors on her behalf.

Scenario 5

Years ago, I remember sitting in a conference room, waiting for my manager to arrive for a weekly staff meeting. One of my colleagues, John, asked me if I was flying to the off-site meeting that night or the next day. I replied with a surprised, "What are you talking about?" John told me that our CEO was hosting a three-day meeting at his vacation compound in Canada, and had invited all the vice presidents. Or so John thought. Clearly, I hadn't made the list.

Acting as a knight, John could have talked to the CEO's assistant and explained why I should be extended a last-minute invitation.

A better action would have been to ask how the invite list was formed, suggest ways to make sure that the process going forward would be fair and unbiased, and help ensure that future meetings would be handled more equitably.

Unfortunately, I don't think John did either of these things. Not only did I not receive a last-minute invitation to that year's off-site meeting, I also wasn't invited the following year either. Nor was another female vice president. To this day, we fondly call each other "chopped liver" and "pond scum" in a show of solidarity.

How to screen your actions

Worried that your good intentions may lead to knight-like behaviors? Use this rubric to screen your actions and responses for savior-style thinking:

- What do I hope to accomplish by doing this?
- How many people will this help?

- How will my action/response change ingrained behaviors within my company?
- If I do/say this, will it matter to anyone a year from now? Five years from now?
- Will this action create equality or equity? Will it remove barriers?

EQUALITY versus EQUITY
Image courtesy of Craig Froehle [17]

There will be times when catalyzing large-scale change within your company or industry will feel impossible, and that's just fine. The goal is to do more and do better as often as you can. Perfection may be impossible, but improvement is well within reach. And on that note ...

Allies do what's right, not what's easy

Often, the knight move is the simplest and the easiest course. It can be tempting to take action quickly so you can feel like you're having a real, measurable impact right away. Let's face it: The working world is fast-paced, and our days are often filled with competing priorities. Plus there are never enough hours in the day. Why bother taking on a big initiative to drive systemic change when I can get something done, check it off my list, and know I helped at least one person?

Because it matters. Because the larger, systemic changes will help shift the ratios in favor of all those who are marginalized under the current systems. Because doing what's right instead of what's easy will lead to a more inclusive workplace where everyone can thrive—and that will result in more innovation, better solutions for customers, and better business results.

In business, we don't need knights in shining armor, but we do need allies to take action and to be ambassadors for change. How will you make sure you're acting as an ally, not a knight? What systemic changes can you institute to create more inclusive workplace cultures—not just for a marginalized individual or two, but for all?

Actions for Better Allies:
Be an Ambassador for Change

Helping individuals is laudable, but the responsibility of allies is to take actions that will have lasting, beneficial effects on systems (as often as possible).

- When lending a hand to a single person, step back to look for systemic changes that will benefit many employees.

- Suggest new processes that will change ingrained behaviors and create a more inclusive culture.

- Pay attention to your motivations: Focus on what will authentically support marginalized people long-term, rather than what will make you feel or look good.

3

LISTENING AND LEARNING

No matter how hard you try or how often you immerse yourself in perspectives other than your own, *you will never be a perfect ally*. None of us will! It's simply not possible to know everything or anticipate the needs and expectations of everyone in our companies or industries. Although this may seem frustrating and overwhelming on the surface, I encourage you to employ an age-old, perception-shifting trick: consider it a challenge instead. A challenge to be curious, to listen and be open-minded, and to iterate as you learn.

We cannot know everything, but we *can* be open to constant learning. We cannot anticipate the needs and expectations of everyone, but we *can* listen when the people around us voice those needs and expectations. We can be respectfully inquisitive, eager to assimilate new information, and ready to alter our ideas and behaviors as needed. Valuable allies ask questions instead of making statements. Valuable allies are agile and willing to reevaluate "the way things are done around here." Valuable allies are on a journey, learning as they go.

What does that mean in action? For starters, it means learning how to discuss discrimination that you have never experienced with someone who experiences it on a regular basis.

How to open the door to learning

There are no two ways about it: Broaching subjects like sexism, racism, harassment, and discrimination in the workplace is hard. These are tough and touchy topics, and many potential allies worry that simply bringing them up may cause rifts. Or that they may say the wrong thing and make the situation worse. This is understandable and worth acknowledging.

However, it is *not* an acceptable excuse for inaction. Remember that true allies take responsibility for learning to do what's right instead of falling back on what's easy. Sparking meaningful change requires pushing past our own fears and being willing to get vulnerable.

What does that vulnerability look like in the field? Here's a great example: On Twitter, I received a direct message from Dave, who had recently taken a leadership role in the allies group at his tech company. He told me he was struggling to figure out where to start, and wondered if I had any suggestions.

I asked, "Do you have specific goals for the group? Have you defined success metrics?"

Well, it turns out that was the heart of the issue. Dave was looking for ideas for good goals, with a focus on educating people on how to be allies, but he was worried about looking like the prototypical white guy telling people about other groups' experiences. He wanted to lead and support and create change, but he didn't want to be cast as an indiscriminate mansplainer.

So I recommended he turn it around, and ask the company's women-in-tech group and other employee resource groups about some of their biggest challenges. From there, he could facilitate a cross-group brainstorming session on how allies could help. For example, those groups might report that they don't have equitable access to mentoring, aren't asked to give presentations at company meetings, aren't invited to attend key customer events, or aren't informed about rotation or stretch assignments. Armed with these insights, Dave could craft a strategy for his allies group to address the areas of need, as well as metrics to measure success.

In other words, he could listen and learn. Instead of guessing at what colleagues from underrepresented groups might need and launching initiatives based on conjecture, he was better served to ask these colleagues *exactly how they wanted to be helped.*

This approach is key to effective allyship. It's inappropriate for allies to assume that they know what's best for an underrepresented group, and that it's potentially harmful to take action on those assumptions. By contrast, let's explore some ways for people in positions of power and/or privilege to open productive discussions with people from underrepresented groups about how they'd like to be supported by allies. If this is you, here are some best practices.

Ask to ask: You'd like to talk with a colleague about their challenges, and that's great! But as someone in a position of privilege, you should ask if your colleague is comfortable and willing to discuss their experiences. Don't assume that they're just waiting to be plied with questions. Ask if they'd be open to a dialogue around discrimination or bias, and *then* dig into your specific questions on the topic.

Acknowledge your fears: Consider opening a dialogue by owning up to your worries about the topic. When you approach a discussion about discrimination by saying, "I'm hoping to get your insights, but am a little concerned about putting my foot in my mouth," you pave the way for honesty. In fact, if you're in a leadership position and choose to be sincere about your imperfections, doubts, and mistakes, you automatically make it safer for others to voice their own feelings and fears.[18]

Be open and respectful: This may seem obvious, but in the context of discrimination discussions, "being open and respectful" may take on some less-than-obvious implications. If you are approaching a member of a marginalized group with questions about their experiences in the workplace, you must be prepared to acknowledge and accept any information they impart. Broadcasting respect means trusting the speaker to share their truth.

For instance, if a woman of color tells you, "My supervisor is far more critical of my grammar than she is of my white colleagues'," and you say, "Oh, that can't be true! Your supervisor is a great leader," you are invalidating and dismissing her perspective. Similarly, as you hear about biased behavior, you may be tempted to respond with a positive spin such as, "I don't think they meant to offend you." Even if your own experience runs counter to what she's telling you, it's your job as an ally to listen and respect her viewpoint. Approaching dialogue from a respectful place helps diffuse tension and create space for meaningful sharing.[19]

Don't get defensive: As you hear about someone else's experience, you may identify things you could have, or should have, done differently to support them directly or to create a more inclusive culture. You may also find yourself getting defensive, which is understandable. Focus on why you are having this conversation (to listen and learn), versus making excuses for your own behavior. (More on this in the next section.)

Apologize: If you realize you made a mistake, don't double down on your stance. Instead, share a heartfelt apology and discuss how you can do better.

Again, these discussions won't be easy, but they are vital to embracing constructive allyship. Dr. Gwendolyn Keita, executive director of the American Psychological Association's Public Interest Directorate, asserts that addressing bias head-on will become increasingly important over time:

> *Human survival may be the most fundamental benefit of eliminating discrimination. That we fear and recoil from those who are different than we are is unfortunate and potentially dangerous. A lack of diversity, perpetuated by discrimination, makes our society weaker. Diversity breeds creative thinking, democratic communities and innovation. Diversity in higher education makes better citizens and results in a more vibrant and prosperous society that benefits everyone. Productive, meaningful dialogues can help contribute significantly to awareness of these important truths.*[20]

How to learn without getting defensive

Opening the door to learning about inequity in our workplaces means that some unexpected feedback may flow through. Asking members of underrepresented groups to share their experiences often leads to candid insights about how people with privilege act and speak, which can cause hackles to rise.

As discussed in Chapter 1, when people who are reminded of their privilege get defensive about it, this is acting in a deeply counterproductive way. It's not about who we are as individuals so much as it is about *which groups we belong to*, and *how those groups are viewed and treated by society*. Perhaps more importantly, pushing back against statements about one's own privilege is one of the quickest ways to shut down communication.

Before I started paying attention to my own privilege, I have to admit I fell into this trap. Years ago, I remember my reaction when hearing someone say, "It's hard for me to get ahead in my career because I don't have a degree from a name-brand university." I found myself thinking, "Well, sure, I went to an Ivy League school, but I did the work to get accepted, took out loans and held a campus job to pay for it, and it wasn't exactly easy to graduate. I worked hard! And now I work just as hard to get ahead in my career." Fortunately, I didn't say any of that out loud. If I had, I bet the conversation would have ended right there.

In order to be an ally, instead of getting defensive I have to graciously accept that I have privilege, receive feedback about my shortcomings, *and* work to assimilate the suggestions I'm given. An essential component of learning is a willingness to change and improve, so I strive to cultivate that within myself and I invite all others striving to be effective allies to do the same. Wondering how? Here are a few ideas:

Embrace your inherent bias: No one is entirely free of prejudice, myself included. It's a tough pill to swallow, but we need to accept that we're all biased due to our own experiences and perspectives. This doesn't make us evil, or hypocritical, or useless in the fight against inequity in the workplace. It just makes us human. But if we deny our inherent biases, we are contributing to systematized inequity on subtle but important levels. And clinging to the idea that we are bias-free prevents us from receiving tough feedback and learning from it.

Know your counter-narratives: On a related note, it's incredibly helpful to know which themes consistently emerge in conversations about gender, race, and other types of discrimination that take place between people with varying amounts of privilege and oppression. If you know the common arguments, you can both understand your own biases and be on alert for biases in those around you.

The Opportunity Agenda, a social justice communication lab, highlights the following common counter-narratives. Although they're framed in terms of racism, they could be applied to sexism, ableism, heterosexism, and other oppressions as well.

- Racism is "largely" over or dying out over time.
- People of color are obsessed with race.
- Alleging discrimination is itself racist and divisive.
- Claiming discrimination is "playing the race card," opportunistic, hypocritical demagoguery.
- Civil rights are a crutch for those who lack merit or drive.
- Racism will always be with us, so it's a waste of time to talk about it.[21]

As Chad Loder, an information security leader, shared with me, "I tell white men: don't go into a conversation to prove a point about gender or race. Instead, ask questions, get people to share their experience, and listen."

Focus on action and improvement: Hearing that you are (or a group you belong to is) doing something wrong is never fun, but without constructive feedback we can never improve. Being an ally means making our workplaces more inclusive and equitable, and that includes changing our own behaviors as needed. If a colleague from an underrepresented group says you constantly interrupt them in meetings, try to set your feelings aside and focus on the action you can take to rectify the situation. What's important here is making change that will create positive ripples into the future.

Why is this important? Because our ability to accept and absorb criticism and feedback has an immeasurable impact on our colleagues from marginalized groups. Robin DiAngelo, author of *White Fragility: Why It's so Hard for White People to Talk about Racism*, is also a facilitator of trainings on racism. In an article for Medium, she shared the following anecdote:

> *In my workshops, I often ask people of color, "How often have you given white people feedback on our unaware yet inevitable racism? How often has that gone well for you?" Eye rolling, head shaking, and outright laughter follow, along with the consensus of rarely, if ever. I then ask, "What would it be like if you could simply give us feedback, have us graciously receive it, reflect, and work to change the behavior?" Recently, a man of color sighed and said, "It would be revolutionary." I ask my fellow whites to consider the profundity of that response. It would be revolutionary if we could receive, reflect, and work to change the behavior.*[22]

It's easy to get defensive. Instead, do the right thing and remain open to difficult feedback.

A guide to red-flag language

Being an ally requires learning about your own ingrained prejudices, but it also requires helping those around us acknowledge theirs. At the risk of entering broken-record territory, *none of us is bias-free* and yet many of us have no idea which biases we exhibit. Furthermore, many people have no idea that certain phrases or assertions reflect personal prejudices.

The following is a list of language that should raise red flags for allies. In other words, when you hear one of these phrases, pay attention and be ready to take action:

- That candidate wouldn't be a culture fit.
- That candidate doesn't have [some qualification that doesn't exist on the job description but that more privileged candidates meet].
- They wouldn't want [cool new role] because of the travel.
- I'd like to see them prove they can handle [responsibility they've already done] before promoting them.
- I don't want to lower the bar.
- There's not enough pipeline to hire more women or people of color.
- [To the only woman in the room] Can you take notes? (More on this one in Chapter 8!)
- I'm not racist/sexist/homophobic, but [some derogatory comment].
- Well, we're different [when hearing about workplace challenges faced by underrepresented groups].
- I've never seen [some form of harassment just reported], so I don't think it could happen here.
- I'm sure they didn't mean to offend anyone.

(This list is far from complete. If you have another phrase that should be red-flagged, please join the conversation at betterallies.com.)

That last one is a doozy. It can be hard for allies to accept that intentions aren't enough, and that words can still be harmful even when spoken in good faith. So let's dive a little deeper into that concept.

How "assuming positive intent" behaves in the wild

It's fairly common for codes of conduct to include a statement about "assuming positive intent" when interacting with others. This mandate is an attempt to curb unproductive conflict and remind participants that everyone involved is trying their best. It's is an idea that comes from a good place, but can unwittingly quash the perspectives of people from underrepresented groups.

Annalee Flower Horne, co-editor at *The Bias*, a website dedicated to diversity and inclusion in tech spaces, explained this issue eloquently, saying:

> *The harm is that telling people to "assume good intent" is a sign that if they come to you with a concern, you will minimize their feelings, police their reactions, and question their perceptions. It tells marginalized people that you don't see codes of conduct as tools to address systemic discrimination, but as tools to manage personal conflicts without taking power differences into account. Telling people to "assume good intent" sends a message about whose feelings you plan to center when an issue arises in your community.*[23]

In essence, including "assume positive intent" in a code of conduct gives careless or ignorant participants a get-out-of-jail-free card; they can say racist or sexist or otherwise inappropriate and harmful things, and just claim that they "didn't mean to be offensive"—that their intent was to learn more, or give an innocuous compliment, or point out something that *seemed* harmless.

This approach also puts people from marginalized groups in the position of "breaking the rules" if they see discriminatory behavior and choose to call it out. They're not "assuming positive intent" when they object; they're seen as being "disruptive" or "overly negative." See how this can cause inherent toxicity?

The mandate to assume positive intent seeps out beyond codes of conduct, too. It can become a blanket excuse for inappropriate workplace behavior of all kinds.

Imagine a white male supervisor who has a Latina assistant. They have a solid relationship overall, but nearly every day he comments on her outfit. His comments are positive, generally along the lines of, "You look gorgeous today!" or "You look great in turquoise. Latinas aren't afraid of bright colors, are they?" His intent may be to boost her confidence in her appearance, but the net effect is that she feels objecttified. If his comments include references to her hair, her curves, or how her choices reflect her culture, she may also feel ethnically pigeonholed.

Now imagine her choices. She can go to HR and say that her boss's daily compliments make her feel uncomfortable, but she risks being scolded for failing to "assume positive intent." Lodging her complaint may ruin her relationship with her supervisor forever, and even make her a pariah among her coworkers. Her other option is to grit her teeth and endure his observations, gradually becoming more frustrated with his well-meaning behavior.

Intent is not valueless, especially because plenty of people do racist and sexist things with full knowledge of how their actions will be received. But intent is not a justification for discrimination. Insisting that colleagues "assume positive intent" can create damaging conditions in a workplace. So instead, let's work to set expectations around *demonstrating* positive intent through respectful action.

Combatting the bystander effect as an ally

Although this chapter is all about listening and learning, listening is not enough when we see biased, offensive, or inappropriate behavior. Listening and keeping quiet doesn't make us neutral, it makes us complicit.

Does coming forward and objecting feel uncomfortable? For many of us, the answer is a resounding, "Heck yes." But this discomfort is nothing compared to how it feels for the person whose racial group is being joked about. Or the colleague who is forced to endure constant commentary about her appearance. Or the coworker who is being excluded due to a disability. The discomfort of allies pales in comparison to what people from marginalized groups are forced to live through on a daily basis.

Let's explore a few situations where allies could have moved from *bystanders* to *upstanders*:

Situation 1

Digital marketing exec Arianna O'Dell described attending a blockchain conference, and while she was sitting in a session a strange man started stroking her thigh.

What happened: When she told a colleague about the incident, his reply was, "It comes with the territory."

What should have happened: Arianna's advice? Her friend "should've confronted the guy: 'Hey, you didn't make my friend feel great just now. You should apologize to her—and keep your hands to yourself.'" If that wasn't possible, a simple "not cool—are you okay?" would have been a good start."[24]

Situation 2

Motivational speaker Tony Robbins commented on the fall 2017 #MeToo movement by sharing the story of a "very powerful man" who told Tony he'd passed over a highly qualified woman for a job because she was "very attractive" and therefore "too big a risk."[25]

What happened: Tony did nothing, apparently believing that this attitude was merited.

What should have happened: Nanine McCool—who was in the audience when these remarks were made, and spoke up against them—advised Tony to "take the time to listen to women who don't agree with you because that's how you learn, that's how you grow." I'd go even further and say that an ally should push back, point out the inherent sexism, and call B.S. Refusing to hire a woman because she's "too attractive" is both chauvinistic and illegal.

Situation 3

A few years back, I met with Pete, an engineering leader in San Francisco, to discuss how to improve diversity in his research lab. As I asked about the office culture and what they did for fun as a team, Pete had a mini a-ha moment. He said, "So, last week, a few guys went to a strip club for lunch. That's probably not a best practice?"

What happened: Pete didn't push back when he heard about the lunchtime outing.

What should have happened: Pete could've pointed out that not everyone feels comfortable going to a strip club, and then recommended a few other lunchtime spots where the entire team could hang out together.

As an ally, how can you equip yourself to confront discrimination and inappropriate behavior when you see it? You can:

- **Be ready:** Start to think of yourself as an Upstander, someone who can and does speak up. Visualize yourself seeing injustice and taking action. Consider queuing up some open-ended responses like, "What makes you feel that way?" or "Why do you say that?" Another idea is a simple, "We don't do that here."
- **Verbalize what you're seeing:** Because many people have no idea that they're biased, sometimes just reflecting back at them jars them into understanding. Point out behavior or language bluntly, but avoid accusations. Try, "Andy, what I hear you saying is that all gay men are overly dramatic." Or, "Susan, you're classifying an entire gender/ethnicity/group in a derogatory way. Is that what you mean to say?"
- **Compare to past behavior:** Letting someone know they're doing something out of character is a great way to alert them to inappropriate behavior. Try appealing to their better instincts with something like, "Jim, I've always thought of you as a fair-minded person. I'm shocked to hear you say something that sounds so bigoted."
- **Set boundaries:** You may not be able to change someone's mind, but you can set limits to their behavior when they're around you. Try, "Don't tell racist jokes in my presence anymore." Or, "I don't tolerate homophobic remarks in my work space. Please respect my wishes."[26]
- See the website Teaching Tolerance (tolerance.org) for more actionable suggestions.

An important "don't": Don't just call someone a racist or sexist or homophobe to their face. "If your goal is to communicate, loaded terms get you nowhere," says Dr. K. E. Supriya, an expert on the role of gender and cultural identity in communication. "If you simply call someone a racist, a wall goes up."[27]

When you see something, do you say something? Do you push back? Do you say, "Not cool" or ask, "Why do you say that?" If not, now's the time to start.

It can happen anywhere

No one wants to believe that their own workplace is oppressive or racist or overflowing with sexist rhetoric. In fact, "That doesn't happen here" is often the default response when leaders are informed about bias within their organization's own walls.

Yet again, defensiveness serves no purpose. Dedicated allies learn to accept that *we are all biased*. Yes, even highly rated, award-winning, utterly delightful workplaces employ people who have prejudices! Yes, even tiny, scrappy start-ups will have ingrained biases! Yes, it absolutely can happen on your home turf.

When Ellen Pao lost her gender discrimination suit against venture capital firm Kleiner Perkins Caufield & Byers in 2015, the *New York Times* approached me to comment. I responded:

> *Many men in [Silicon] Valley genuinely believe that their company is a meritocracy. They think that the gender problem is something that happens somewhere else. It's my sincere hope that because Kleiner is so well known, they'll see that this problem is not at the corner. It's at the heartbeat. And after*

this, we'll have a series of cautionary tales about what not to do going forward.[28]

When leaders refuse to believe that bad behavior is happening under their own roofs, they do their organizations a disservice. Their denial prevents them from learning and growing, from addressing issues that negatively affect the women, people of color, and other people from marginalized groups who work so hard for the communal success of their organizations. If leaders fall into patterns of denial, their companies may garner reputations as workplaces that are unfriendly to workers from underrepresented groups, and they will have increasing difficulty hiring a diverse workforce. It's a domino effect that leads to a nasty cascade of repercussions.

So, instead, if you are in a position of privilege, resist the urge to say, "That doesn't happen here." Especially if your employees or coworkers come forward and tell us that *it does.* Instead of steadfastly and stubbornly insisting that our companies are already as equitable as they can be, work hard to make them even better.

Want some quick tips on how to kick-start that process? Here are three:

1. **Listen:** Spend an entire day attempting to ask questions of your colleagues instead of making statements (as often as possible!). What did you learn? How did it feel?
2. **Believe:** The next time someone tells you a story or piece of information that makes you balk, pause. Count to five and evaluate *why* you have doubts.
3. **Learn:** If you have a close relationship with a member of an underrepresented group in your company, ask if they'd be comfortable discussing inequities in your shared workplace. If they agree, ask,

"How can I change my own behaviors to be more supportive?"

Allies never stop learning

When it comes to spotting other allies, here's your biggest tip-off: They're the ones humbly and eagerly asking the tough questions. They're the ones who are quick to hold themselves accountable when they screw up. They're the ones who listen compassionately and learn constantly. Those are the people you want to seek out, the people you want to observe and emulate.

Allyship involves lots of advocacy and action, but it's all built on a foundation of listening and learning. When aspiring allies charge ahead making changes and revising policies, it isn't long before they lose sight of the real goals. If we truly want to help shift the balance of power and fully support people from marginalized groups, it is absolutely crucial to continually solicit and incorporate *their* feedback about the issues that *they* want addressed. Skip that key step, and allyship is hollow and meaningless. Listen. Learn. Iterate. Repeat. Doing this will imbue your actions with meaning and value, now and into the future.

Actions for Better Allies:
Listen, Believe, Learn

Being an effective ally includes the less forceful but equally important activities of listening to alternate perspectives, accepting the information that people from underrepresented groups share, and learning from their stories and one's own mistakes.

- Be vulnerable and honest when you open discussions with colleagues who have less power and privilege than you.

- Resist the urge to get defensive.

- Review the list of red-flag phrases that was included in this chapter, and speak out when you hear them.

- Take action when you see or hear about bigotry, harassment, or discrimination. Be an upstander, not a bystander.

- Accept that yes, prejudice does exist in your own workplace.

PART TWO

SUBTLE SHIFTS AND SUPPORTIVE BEHAVIORS

4

YOUR NETWORK

In 2012, I made a big career decision. After spending more than twenty-five years building software products and working for prominent tech companies, I decided to strike out on my own. I was fed up with the lack of gender diversity in the software industry, and I wanted to help keep women in tech, if that's where they wanted to be. So, I created a business to advocate for women and help them advance their careers. I became a leadership coach for women.

Starting my business was, in a word, daunting. I had never run a small business. I didn't know the first thing about marketing, attracting clients, pricing my services, or closing deals.

So I turned to my network for advice. But there was a problem: I hadn't invested much time in building or nurturing it. Sure, I had my fair share of connections on LinkedIn, but many of those were distant or dormant. My network was limited and frankly a bit stale, and I knew I needed to spend time shoring it up.

I started looking for networking events to attend, and uncovered lots of opportunities. Women in Tech meetups. Girl

Geek dinners. Women Who Code events. The Women's CLUB of Silicon Valley. Armed with my new business cards that declared me to be an "advocate for women in tech," I started networking like a champ. Or so I thought.

I met a lot of people, but I have to admit that my network-building strategy was flawed. My goal was to meet women working in tech to build awareness of my new coaching practice and hopefully land some business. I was going for a high volume of connections, assuming that the more women I met, the more clients I could book. A few engagements did shake out of my initial efforts, but, in hindsight, I should have been more strategic about who I was adding to my network. Instead of focusing on technical women like myself, I should have been targeting engineering leaders who could bring me in to coach their employees. Frankly, I also should have been networking with men in positions of power.

With my flawed strategy, I built a highly homogeneous network. It was full of mostly women, who, as it turned out, were mostly white. Just like me.

How to spot a truly effective network (hint: it's diverse)

Did you know most people have largely homogenous professional networks? As I learned from a report from the Kapor Center for Social Impact, for example, 75 percent of white people don't have any people of color in their social network.[29] And, according to the 2017 "Women in the Workplace" study by LeanIn.Org and McKinsey & Company: "Women are more than five times more likely to rely on a network that is mostly female."[30]

Homogeneous networks form because of the way we network. Herminia Ibarra, a professor of organizational behavior at the London Business School, says, "Left to our own devices ... we produce networks that are 'just like me,' convenience networks."[31]

This makes sense, because common interests tend to fuel networks. Let's face it, we meet new people because of our shared hobbies or other interests. At Adobe, I joined the knitting club in our San Francisco office. Meeting over lunch on Wednesdays, we got to know each other while knitting baby blankets and hats for a local nonprofit. I loved it. But, guess how many male colleagues I met via the knitting group? Zero. Sure, there are men who enjoy knitting, but none joined our group.

Building a professional network across lines of difference can prove difficult, especially when it involves getting outside our comfort zone. While not impossible, it can be challenging. Outside of work, men tend to hang out with their male coworkers, perhaps grabbing a beer after work, playing poker or a round of golf, or going to a ball game together. By contrast, women are more likely to spend time with non-work friends outside of the office, such as book club members, fellow volunteers for a nonprofit, members of a religious organization, or, if we have kids, other parents from playgroups and school.[32] For women who handle the lion's share of housework and childcare, networking can be extra challenging. Home responsibilities can make it tough to pull off attending evening events or out-of-town conferences.

The upshot: Men network with men, women with women. Engineers network with other engineers, and marketers with other marketers. We want people who understand us, and instinctively know that people who are similar to us are likely to relate to our challenges and triumphs. It's human nature.

It's also counterproductive. Talking among ourselves creates an echo chamber effect, and limits our access to other perspectives, experiences, and resources. Networking with people in our own fields and/or who share our same gender identities, ethnicities, educational backgrounds, and income brackets, for example, allows us to vent and swap stories, but it doesn't encourage us to learn about wildly different experiences. And it certainly doesn't open our minds to the struggles that people with different and more marginalized experiences than us face in their lives and careers.

Ivan Misner, who developed more than three thousand networking groups in sixteen countries around the world, told *Entrepreneur*:

> *Some of the strongest networking groups I've seen over the past two decades are ones that are diverse in many ways. They have a good mix of members based not only on race and gender, but also on profession, age, education and experience. The more diverse your network, the more likely you are to make overlapping linkages between clusters of people. The more linkages you can make between clusters of people, the stronger your network can be.*[33]

Our personal networks benefit from diversity, too. In a *Harvard Business Review* article by Paul Gompers and Silpa Kovvali titled "The Other Diversity Dividend," I read about the importance of building diverse friend networks. It turns out that friendships across lines of ethnicity and sexual orientation reduce implicit bias. And these benefits carry over to work, where expanded networks and mindsets can improve individual and organizational performance.[34] Obvious? Maybe, but how many of us actually do this?

I'm hoping that, in the future, more people will reach beyond their comfort zones and push themselves to network with people who aren't "like" them. Doing this both expands our available opportunities and expands our minds.

Networking in the #MeToo era

Since the recent media reports of sexual harassment, almost half of male managers are uncomfortable participating in a common work activity with a woman, such as mentoring, working alone, or socializing together. — LeanIn.Org[35]

If you read the previous section and found yourself thinking, "But, I'm a guy. How on earth do I network across gender identities in *this* climate? One wrong word, joke, or choice, and I'll get thrown into the penalty box!" You might be scared you'll get fired, be sued, or ruin your career.

This is a *somewhat* understandable reaction. Research by LeanIn.Org found that men in senior leadership roles are now 3.5 times more likely to feel uncertain about scheduling a work dinner with a junior-level woman than with a junior-level man.[36] And according to the Pew Research Center, 51 percent of Americans believe the #MeToo movement has made it harder for men to know how to interact with women in the workplace.[37] This dynamic feels new to many men, and many men are unsure how to navigate it without feeling fearful and vulnerable.

Many have even adopted something called "the Billy Graham rule" or "the Mike Pence rule." This is a practice where a male leader avoids spending time alone with any woman who isn't his wife. Regardless of the motivation behind it, this rule is a real thing and it has real consequences for women and their ability to advance under male supervisors. There are both corporations and individuals who have adopted it.[38]

I've met some of these men. A business unit leader once announced during a workshop I was facilitating, "My wife gets jealous when I have a work dinner with a female coworker," and then asked, "How should I handle that?" My snarky side wanted to scream at him to go to couples' therapy. Instead, I simply recommended, "You could always bring along another coworker. Or only meet coworkers of any gender over breakfast." I'm hoping that the discussion had an impact—if not on him, then at least on the rest of the attendees.

This "Mike Pence rule" has been growing in popularity since the #MeToo movement began. In early 2018, LeanIn.Org and SurveyMonkey surveyed almost three thousand employed adults about harassment. As the quote above points out, nearly half of male managers said that since #MeToo, they're now uncomfortable working alone, mentoring, or socializing with a woman—twice as many as before the #MeToo movement started. That's a substantial change in attitude in only a few months.[39]

I'm disturbed by this trend. No one should be excluded from out-of-the-office activities where colleagues get to know each other, share ideas, and learn from each other. In an interview in *The Atlantic*, Kim Elsesser, a professor of psychology and gender at UCLA, shared an example that caught my attention:

> *A boss has season tickets to see a baseball team. He generally invites men from work to join him—not because of discrimination, but because he's worried about how the invitation would be perceived if he extended it to a woman. So he invites male coworkers to the baseball game, and they discuss work—clients and upcoming projects. The boss hears these male employees' ideas, and that gives them an advantage in the workplace. As time goes by, he gives them opportunities the women just don't get.*
>
> *Over time, men get to know other men much better and women get to know other women much better. Men run most of our companies, and therefore they tend to be the most valuable*

mentors. When a promotion or a new job opportunity comes up, the man chooses the person that he knows slightly better—the person he had that beer with. Over time, this can have major repercussions.[40]

Well said.

It may feel increasingly uncomfortable and complex for male leaders to be active allies to their female colleagues and employees, but shying away from interacting with women in the workplace doesn't make it any easier. And while avoiding women altogether may make some men feel more comfortable, it also has the toxic side effect of further isolating and ostracizing women in the workplace. The #MeToo movement is not meant to drive a giant wedge between people of different genders when it comes to professional networking and mentoring, but if men take a giant step back, it will.

So if you are a male leader, first of all, don't become part of this trend. Check yourself often. Reflect back on your week and ask yourself if you avoided being alone with a co-worker because of concerns that they, or others, might think it was more than a professional interaction. If the answer is "yup" or "well, maybe," there's work to do.

Next, be open and honest about your concerns. If you want to chat with a woman colleague over coffee instead of in a stale, airless conference room but worry she might take it the wrong way, say so. Try, "How would you feel about meeting downstairs at the cafe for this meeting? If you'd be more comfortable in the office, that's completely fine, too. I just thought a change of scene might be nice." Offer choices, offer an out, and you'll show the other person that their input is welcome and they're not powerless.

Finally, become a role model for others. As the LeanIn. Org team recommends to men, mentor a woman. Informally or formally, it can make a difference. Respond to that next email seeking your advice. Tell the women's group at your company you are available to be a mentor. Volunteer through a formal mentoring program.

By the way, mentoring is a two-way street. By sharing our experiences and advice with others, we have the opportunity to help them grow in their careers. At the same time, we can learn from them and grow in our own careers. This may be the most compelling reason why we *shouldn't* embrace "the Mike Pence rule."

Can allies attend identity-specific networking events?

I've made the case for diversifying our networks above. But if we naturally segregate by gender or race, this can prove difficult. If a man is actively seeking to increase the number of women in his professional network, is it okay for him to attend a women's event? Similarly, is it okay for a white person to attend an event for people of color?

In March of 2017, I ran a brief Twitter poll asking for perspectives on men attending women's events. I also asked meeting organizers about their policies and did some searching online. Not surprisingly, both pros and cons surfaced.

First, the pros. By attending a women's conference, event, or meeting, men can:

- Demonstrate support for women
- Learn from the presentations and the conversations and better understand how to be an ally
- Build empathy for what it's like to be a member of an underrepresented group
- Diversify their networks
- Spot talent for job openings at their company

And there's an upside for women when men attend these events. Women can:

- Diversify their networks with male colleagues or industry contacts
- Cultivate sponsors for their own career growth or for diversity initiatives
- Foster stronger allies for themselves and their peers

On the flip side, some women's events sell out quickly. Why should a man take a seat that would otherwise go to a deserving woman? Furthermore, many women's events, especially smaller ones, are designed to create a safer space for women to discuss their concerns. Having men in the room might constrain the dialogue, especially if those concerns are *about* men. These same concerns surface for events tailored to other underrepresented groups. Why should a white person get to show up in a space created for people of color to discuss the issues that affect them? If a cisgender individual attends a trans event, the rest of the attendees may feel uncomfortable being totally candid.

Some women responded to my Twitter poll by pointing out a few issues specific to men infiltrating women's events. In short, they may be seen as having questionable motives. A sampling of quotes includes: "Guys at professional events are always hitting on me"; "They just want to check a box on their personal diversity scorecard"; and "They're annoying: desperate to find candidates to increase their company's diversity ratio."

Clearly this is not a cut-and-dried issue, but even in light of these concerns, I believe that allies have a lot to gain from attending certain kinds of events for underrepresented groups (the ones with open discussions, versus those designed to create safe spaces for discussion) and that such groups

benefit when allies participate. I also believe that there are
three boxes that should be checked if you're a person with
substantial privilege and you'd like to attend a gathering that's
been specifically organized for people who are marginalized
in a way that you are not. Make sure:

- You'll be welcome (Not sure? Ask the organizer, and
  respect their response.)
- You're clear on your intentions (My suggestion? To
  become a better ally.)
- You're prepared to listen and learn

Simple as that.

How to diversify your network: Getting started

"Just like me" networks can have a negative impact on creating diverse, inclusive workplaces. Those who are involved in
hiring new staff naturally look to the people who are part of
their professional networks, because they know and trust
them, but when those networks are homogenous, this translates to favoring and advocating for folks like themselves. Depending on referrals is standard, and if those referrals come
from a homogeneous network, it results in just hiring more
homogeneity. It's also common for leaders to favor their
network members when assigning career-advancing stretch
goals, reviewing candidates for promotions and key spots
during reorganizations, and creating succession plans. We instinctively bolster the people we know and trust, who are
almost always, without fail, people just like us.

As of the writing of this book, white men still hold the
majority of senior-level positions in U.S. companies across all
sorts of industries. And because white men generally have
networks brimming with other white men, this means

women, people of color, and members of other underrepresented groups are less likely to have access to the people
who can help them boost their careers.[41]

In other words, if you only open doors to people in your
network, chances are they'll be for people who are similar to
you. If you've read this far, you'll undoubtedly recognize that
to be problematic (or so I hope!). Luckily, diversifying your
network isn't the onerous task you may fear it to be. There
are many simple, easy actions that can be taken to widen your
professional circle outside your comfort zone.

The next time you're grabbing coffee at the office, or attending an event or conference:

- Reach out to people who don't look like you.
  Introduce yourself to someone of a different gender,
  race, age, or other visible difference. Get to know
  them and stay in touch with them. Perhaps you'll be
  able to learn from them or introduce them to a career
  opportunity down the road.

- Attend industry events for people who are different
  from you. Each is an opportunity to listen and learn
  about their experiences, and of course to expand your
  network. Not sure if you'd be welcome? Check the
  event information or ask the organizer. Many such
  groups and gatherings are open to allies.

- Volunteer for an organization that serves a diverse
  populace, or operates outside your own neighborhood.

- Try a conference on a topic that isn't your exact area
  of expertise. Attend any panels that feature a diversity
  of speakers, and make sure to connect with other
  attendees.

- At every company event, networking opportunity, and
  industry party, force yourself to talk to one total

stranger who is different from you. Just walk up,
introduce yourself, and ask them what they're working
on right now that excites them.

Of course, there are also many ways to expand and diversify your connections online. Consider:

- Joining Slack channels for underrepresented groups
  (after asking first if you'd be welcome)
- Listening to a variety of podcasts by or featuring
  people from marginalized communities
- Following people of different genders, ethnic
  backgrounds, ages, abilities, and so forth on social
  media

If you're ready to make an even bigger move outside your
comfort zone, offer to mentor someone who is a member of
a marginalized group. This will give you the opportunity to
both learn *and* teach, as well as grow *and* foster the growth of
another.

Actions for Better Allies:
Diversify Your Network

Most of us have largely homogeneous networks. Here are some tips for ensuring that your network is diverse and more effective:

- Do a network inventory. List out the people you feel to be your top ten contacts. Are any of them marginalized in ways that you are not? If not, start in your own backyard: Who within your own company could be a great addition to your current network?

- Attend an event where diversity will be the topic of discussion. Listen and learn.

- The next time you attend an event of *any* kind, introduce yourself to someone who doesn't look like you.

- If you are interested in attending an event that caters specifically to a group of which you are not a member, ask the organizers before showing up.

- Seek out media, including podcasts and blogs, by people who are different from you.

ORGANIZING AND ATTENDING EVENTS

Imagine attending a party at a conference. You've had a long day of participating in group sessions, networking with colleagues, and absorbing tons of information. You're just scoping out the room to see if anyone you know has already arrived when some stranger hands you their empty plate to be cleared. Or asks you to get them another drink. If you're a person of color, you might not have to use your imagination, because you might very well have had this experience yourself. I've heard from engineers of color that they've been mistaken for members of the catering staff at events they attend. One turban-clad software engineer told me it happened to him at a reception, even though he was wearing a tuxedo—another guest approached him and asked him to refill one of the buffet items.

Now imagine meeting someone at the party and the first words out of their mouth are, "Do you work in HR?" If you're a woman, you've most likely lost count of the number of times this has happened to you. I've experienced this one firsthand: Not too long ago, I visited my partner Tim at his new office in San Francisco. As he gave me a tour, he introduced me to some of his colleagues. It was great to put some faces to the names I'd been hearing over dinner since he started a few months earlier. What wasn't so great was meeting one man in particular, who said, "I hear you used to work at Adobe. So, did you work in HR or Marketing?"

I felt like growling at him, but instead I bit my lip and replied, "Actually, I was a vice president of engineering."

Perhaps people in your very own office assume that you're not in a technical role. As one woman shared via Twitter, "The chief technology officer said to me, 'What do you do here? Business analyst?' I was a developer with an award on the wall behind him." Now, there's absolutely nothing wrong with working in HR or being a business analyst or holding any other non-technical role. It's the implication that women *never* work in technical roles that really burns.

Here's another scenario: You're sipping a cocktail at the post-conference party and chatting with a guy from another company. He asks how you ended up attending, then looks astounded when you say, "I'm one of the speakers."

I hear these stories all too often from members of marginalized groups—stories where people with deep expertise are presumed not to have any. Where others make the wrong assumptions about them, over and over again. Where people from underrepresented groups get subtle (and overt) messages that they don't belong.

It's a thing, and it adds up. It's like death by a thousand cuts. Only it's a thousand microaggressions doing the damage.

Understanding and combatting microaggressions

Never heard the term "microaggression" before? You're not alone. What the term describes has existed for hundreds of years, but it has only carried this particular label since the 1970s. Columbia University psychology professor Derald Wing Sue, PhD, defines the term as follows:

> *Microaggressions are the everyday verbal, nonverbal, and environmental slights, snubs, or insults, whether intentional or unintentional, which communicate hostile, derogatory, or negative messages to target persons based solely upon their marginalized group membership. In many cases, these hidden messages may invalidate the group identity or experiential reality of target persons, demean them on a personal or group level, communicate they are lesser human beings, suggest they do not belong with the majority group, threaten and intimidate, or relegate them to inferior status and treatment.*[42]

Sounds pretty awful, right? Anyone who's been on the receiving can confirm that *it is*. In fact, for some people, microaggressions are harder to bear than more overt bigotry because they're subtle but ever-present, small but ongoing. They wear a person down slowly over time, like dripping water on a stone, gradually convincing them that they're less-than, through barely noticeable social cues and offhand remarks.

Here are some examples of microaggressions that surface frequently in workplaces:

- **You've got the wrong room. This is the engineers/managers meeting.** Just like at the hypothetical party above, it's fairly common for people to assume that people from underrepresented groups couldn't possibly hold development-focused or leadership roles.

- **Where are you *really* from?** When people of color are asked this, it implies that they can't possibly be a "real" American. Or worse, that they don't "belong" in this country.

- **Oops! Wrong person.** When there are only two people of color, women, queer people, Muslims, or members of another underrepresented group at a meeting, event, or company, odds are good that someone will get them mixed up, sending the message that they "all look the same" and aren't seen as individuals.

- **Your English is so good/you're so articulate.** Why are you surprised? Because the person has a non-Anglo name? Because of their skin color?

- **You look so young!** This implies that you're surprised the person in question is experienced or seasoned, which undermines their authority. In addition, if the recipient is a woman, it puts focus squarely on her appearance instead of her accomplishments.[43]

Many of these may seem harmless; some even masquerade as compliments. Many of them are handed out by well-meaning people who have no idea that they're being condescending or marginalizing. But effective allies must learn to be aware of microaggressions like these so they can avoid them at all costs.

How can you do that? Here are some strategies:

- **Accept that microaggressions are real:** If you haven't been on the receiving end of this behavior, you may feel like the people describing it are "exaggerating" its effects. They're not. Denying the existence and power of microaggressions is counterproductive. Believe people when they say they're being adversely affected.

- **Create a forum for discussion:** The best way to root out an insidious problem is to shine a bright light on it. Consider hosting events or discussion groups to highlight microaggressions, teach people how to spot them, and train them to avoid the associated behaviors.[44]

- **Stand up against microaggressions:** Once you know how to spot one, speak up when you witness one. (More on this later in this chapter.)

Professional events are rife with microaggressions against underrepresented groups, and plenty of them foster more overtly harmful behaviors, too. Everyone from organizers to attendees can end up making people from marginalized groups feel unwelcome, targeted, unseen, or even objectified. Want to avoid hosting (or attending) conferences and gatherings that allow prejudiced activities and language? Then read on!

How to make professional events more inclusive

Whether you're booking speakers, choosing menus, delivering a keynote, or simply attending as a participant, you can help make conferences, meetings, and other gatherings more welcoming to all attendees.

1. Utilize a diverse planning committee

A diverse planning committee is one of the best ways to create an inclusive event. Make sure that the planning and leadership of the event includes women, people of color,

LGBTQ people, people with disabilities, and other people from underrepresented groups.

2. Make sure events feature diverse voices

In early 2018, the RSA security conference announced their 2018 speaker lineup: Nineteen keynotes by men, and only one by a woman. To make matters worse, the female keynote speaker was Monica Lewinsky, who would speak not about technology but about "The Price of Shame." Out of frustration with the lineup, the OURSA conference was born. (Notice the clever play on words? Organizers reclaimed the topic by naming their gathering "our" SA.)

At OURSA, every single speaker was from a background that is typically underrepresented in the privacy and security field—and it was organized in record time. Clearly these voices were out there, ready, willing, and more than able to share their technical expertise. A diverse organizing committee invited and attracted a diverse set of speakers. Those speakers, in turn, attracted a diverse group of attendees. And that led to an inclusive event.

If you're organizing an event and are having trouble identifying speakers from underrepresented groups, here are two suggestions: Diversify your network (following some of the tips in Chapter 4), and ask *every white male speaker* to recommend at least one person from an underrepresented group to deliver a talk.

If you're considering attending an event but see a lineup of speakers that's overwhelmingly homogeneous, contact the organizers and ask about it. Suggest people from your own network who could be swapped in or contacted for future speaking opportunities (after asking them first if they'd like to be recommended).

3. Create a code of conduct

Everyone deserves to feel comfortable and safe within a community. A code of conduct is one indicator that the organizers of a conference or other event want to provide a harassment-free experience for everyone.

Before accepting a speaking engagement or registering for an event, ask if there's a code of conduct. Of course, it's not enough for there to just be a code of conduct. It also needs to be enforced. Ask about that, too. (More on this later in this chapter.)

4. Make sure events are fully accessible

If an event is being held in the United States, it's likely that the rented space already complies with the Americans with Disabilities Act (ADA), but there's so much more that's needed in order to make an event truly inclusive. Many disabilities are invisible and others are not related to physical needs, but all merit respect and accommodation. Are ramps clearly marked? Are pathways wide enough that people with wheelchairs and scooters can navigate them? Is type large and high-contrast? Will simultaneous sign language translation and closed captions be offered? The ADA offers a comprehensive document titled "A Planning Guide for Making Temporary Events Accessible to People with Disabilities" online.[45] It's definitely worth a look.

Planning an event and not sure what accommodations you should provide? On your event registration form, provide a point of contact and invite attendees to let you know their needs in advance—and be sure to be prepared to respond to and meet whatever needs attendees specify.

5. Feature a diversity of people in slides and media

We send subtle messages whenever and wherever we use images. In presentations and pitch decks. In user personas. In marketing collateral. In blog posts. On websites. If these materials show only white people, or men, or people with no visible disabilities, for example, it reinforces stereotypes.

It may be understated, but the simple act of using stock photos that feature people of color and other underrepresented groups makes a difference. Seeing someone who looks like you in the promotions for a conference or event is a clear signal that people who look like you will be welcome. Representation matters. Need some sources? Check out the "Additional Resources" section at the end of this book for a list of stock photography sites featuring people from underrepresented groups.

6. Provide financial assistance

To encourage and support a diverse group of attendees, consider providing scholarships, travel stipends, or lower registration rates to people from underrepresented groups. Think about offering child care services at no charge, like the Grace Hopper Celebration of Women in Computing started doing a few years ago.

7. Offer mocktails with those cocktails

Imagine an event where the only available food is pepperoni pizza. Imagine this is the case because pepperoni pizza is traditionally served at all industry parties. Now imagine being lactose intolerant, someone who keeps kosher, a vegetarian or vegan, or someone with celiac disease. If you knew that you'd have no other choices besides pepperoni pizza, would you ever attend events? If you did, would you feel welcome? What if you *just didn't like* pepperoni pizza?

Think you might get tired of explaining that every time a colleague offered you a slice?

This is a bit of an extreme example, but goes a long way toward highlighting the plight of the non-drinker. There are myriad reasons someone might choose not to drink alcohol, including religious, age-related, pregnancy, addiction, and medical reasons. Additionally, some people might not want to get buzzed or *just don't like* alcohol! Absolutely none of these reasons are anyone's business, and absolutely none of them are legitimate excuses for making an event attendee feel ostracized or left out.

If there's a budget for fancy cocktails and craft beers, there's a budget for mocktails, kombucha, bubble tea, and so forth. Planning an inclusive event when it comes to beverages means providing an equal number and quality of alcoholic and non-alcoholic drink options. That's right, canned soda and orange juice from concentrate won't cut it. The point is to make non-drinkers feel like valued equals, not second-class citizens.[46]

8. Look holistically at the experience

Yup, it's 2019 and I'm here stating what should be obvious. Sexualized, pinup images don't belong on swag or any professional material. It's offensive and derogatory toward women. And yet at the 2018 InfoSec World conference, Security Weekly handed out a bumper sticker that said "code naked" with a pinup silhouette (there were T-shirts, too).

As someone said in an online discussion about the sticker, "I might have thought those were awesome … when I was 14." Spot on.

As an organizer, think holistically about the experience people will have at your event: the conference theme, talk titles, and even playlists used between speakers or leading up to a plenary address. I heard from someone who attended the LGBTQ Task Force's national Creating Change conference and, right before a panel discussion on HIV/AIDS, the dance song "Die Young" by Kesha was played. It was horrifically insensitive.

9. Review the speakers' slides

If you're an event organizer and have the opportunity to review slides before your event, look out for risqué, insensitive, or offensive content.

During the summer of 2018, while giving an acceptance speech for a distinguished award, a researcher showed several pictures of "scantily clad female students" doing field research. As the Rochester *Democrat and Chronicle* reported, "The photographs were risqué enough that conference organizers added blue boxes to cover parts of the women's bodies."[47]

Better would have been to reject the slides completely.

10. Gather feedback

After an event, many organizers send out brief surveys to get feedback and look for ways to improve it the next time. Why not also ask if the event could have been more inclusive, and if so, how?

When you see something, say something

Professional events are where people from across an industry gather to meet, exchange ideas, and network. When conferences and events feel unwelcoming or hostile to members of marginalized groups, they are less likely to engage or attend. This translates to excluding them from some of the most important connection opportunities in the field, preventing them from forging valuable relationships and advancing their careers. And this, in turn, means that people who choose to say nothing after witnessing microaggressions, offensive jokes, or other inappropriate behavior at events are enabling this phenomenon. We become complicit. There is no neutral. It's our duty as allies to speak up.

Of course, "speaking up" is never easy. Western society trains us to avoid confrontation and conflict, so marching up to someone who just dropped a racist remark and saying, "That's not okay" can feel deeply uncomfortable. Before digging into actionable strategies, here's a quick reminder about in-person callouts: They involve words. Just words. Telling someone they're acting like a jerk at a conference doesn't hold the same risks as relaying that same message to a drunk person at a bar. You are unlikely to come to blows. In fact, it's probable that the worst that'll happen is some social awkwardness and tense silence. You can survive this. You can do this. The mere fact that most people aren't brave enough to confront bigoted behavior means that *when you do*, it is likely to have a huge impact.

So how do you go about it? The easiest way is simply to have some scripted responses in your back pocket. In the moment, you might freeze up and doubt yourself, so memorizing a few stock callouts is a great way to prepare yourself to confront inappropriate behavior.

Responses to witnessing microaggressions

- **"What makes you say/think that?"** See someone telling a Latina that her "English is fantastic"? Ask them why they're mentioning it. Force them to examine their motives and mental connections.
- **"I'd like to hear the rest of what ___ was saying."** This is a useful response to interruptions.
- **"That made me feel uncomfortable."**

Responses to offensive jokes

- **"I don't get it. Can you explain the joke to me?"** Again, this forces the speaker to dig into their reasoning aloud, which brings bigotry to light.
- **"That wasn't funny."**
- **"That's against our code of conduct."** Naturally, only use this one in cases where there is an actual code in place.
- **"Wow, that was awkward."**
- **"Did you really just say that?"**
- **"Actually, that's a really bad stereotype."**

Responses to social or physical harassment

- **"Everything okay here?"** Just checking in verbally with someone who looks uncomfortable can be the equivalent of throwing them a lifeline.
- **"Not cool."** Notice someone flirting or getting physically close to a woman (and sensing that it's unwanted)? Call it out with these simple words.
- **"We don't do that here."** A useful phrase for enforcing cultural norms that are inclusive.

When witnessing offensive, harmful, or harassing behavior of any kind, each of us has a simple choice: Call it out or be complicit. It's important to note that this applies even if no one present is personally offended or targeted by it.

How to craft a useful code of conduct

Because most of the problematic behaviors at events aren't illegal, and because many are subtle and social in nature, it can be helpful to write, publish, and enforce rules specific to an event. When it comes to curbing microaggressions and harassment, a code of conduct can make a huge difference.

The purpose of a code of conduct is to protect members of a community from harm by other members of the community, even if that harm is unintended. In fact, thoughtful and impactful codes of conduct address behaviors that the general population may view as socially acceptable but which are unacceptable within a particular community, group, or professional context.

Here's an example from tech company Mapbox:

Events Code of Conduct

All attendees, speakers, sponsors, vendors, partners and volunteers at our conferences/events are required to adhere to the following Code of Conduct. Mapbox event organizers will enforce this Code throughout the event.

Our aim in hosting events is to build community. To that end, our goal is to create an environment where everyone feels welcome to participate, speak up, ask questions, and engage in conversation. We invite all those who participate in this event to help us create safe and positive experiences for everyone.

Every Mapbox event/conference is dedicated to providing a harassment-free environment for everyone, regardless of gender, gender identity and expression, age, sexual orientation, disability, physical appearance, body size, race, ethnicity, or religion (or lack thereof). We do not tolerate harassment of participants in any form. Sexual language and imagery is not appropriate during any aspect of the event/conference, including talks, workshops, parties, social media such as Twitter, or other online media.

Expected Behavior

- Participate in an authentic and active way. In doing so, you contribute to the health and longevity of the community.

- Exercise consideration and respect in your speech and actions.

- Attempt collaboration before conflict.

- Refrain from demeaning, discriminatory, or harassing behavior and speech.

- Be mindful of your surroundings and of your fellow participants. Alert community leaders if you notice a dangerous situation, someone in distress, or violations of this Code of Conduct, even if they seem inconsequential.

Conference participants violating these rules may be sanctioned or expelled from the event/conference without a refund at the discretion of the organizers. Participants asked to stop any harassing behavior are expected to comply immediately.

Reporting an Incident

If you see, overhear or experience a violation of the Code of Conduct during an event, please seek out the nearest Mapbox team member to escalate your complaint. If you cannot find a team member, or would like to report a violation after an event, you may email events@mapbox.com.[48]

Note the essential components:

- A statement that the event organizers will not tolerate certain behaviors
- A description of the inappropriate behaviors and who they might target
- An explanation of the possible actions or sanctions that will be taken against offenders
- Directions on what to do if one experiences or sees unacceptable behavior
- A list of the ways the organizers will support anyone who has been targeted
- Indication that anyone unwilling to comply should not attend

Codes of conduct can be considerably more detailed if there is a need, which may be the case for events with a history of some specific kind of inappropriate behavior. However, all that's really needed are these six elements to create a clear, enforceable code of conduct.

Valerie Aurora, principal consultant at Frame Shift Consulting, points out that there are several elements that should be *omitted* from codes of conduct. Don't call out behaviors that aren't common in a community (e.g., juggling in the aisles during events) and don't call out crimes or behaviors that are universally unacceptable (e.g., stealing money). Doing this distracts from what's essential about the code and insults your attendees. Don't mandate politeness or other forms of "proper" behavior, as these are deeply subjective, difficult to enforce, and often serve to further marginalize underrepresented groups. Finally, don't list rules that won't or can't be enforced. Codes of conduct must be backed up with action.[49]

Speaking of which, Valerie points out that offenders should not be taken aside and chastised or hidden from view. She says, "Visible enforcement is required! People want secret enforcement to avoid drawing attention to themselves or others. If no one sees the consequences of violating the code of conduct, more people will violate the code of conduct. It's impossible to set norms secretly or without embarrassing people occasionally."[50]

A code of conduct needs to prove that actions have consequences. It will only be an effective tool for protecting conference attendees and participants if everyone knows for sure that it will be enforced.

Allies can help enforce codes of conduct. Allies can and should work harder to ensure that the events they sponsor and attend feel safe for all, including underrepresented groups. Right now, discussion of tech events is brimming with appalling stories about harassment, sexism, racism, and microaggressions. Beyond tech, the news is full of stories about members of marginalized groups feeling threatened, demeaned, disrespected, or worse in their places of work. Together, we can force those numbers downward until professsional gatherings become the welcoming, equitable, uplifting events they ought to be.

Actions for Better Allies:
Make Events Welcoming

Too many professional events can be inhospitable for members of underrepresented groups. Here are some ways to help turn the tide:

- Make events inclusive. Feature diverse voices, offer interesting non-alcoholic drinks, create and enforce a code of conduct, practice full accessibility, provide financial assistance, and push back on risqué images and offensive swag.

- Before attending or agreeing to speak at an event, make sure there will be a code of conduct as well as other support for attendees from underrepresented groups.

- If you see a lineup of speakers that's homogeneous, contact the organizers and demand better.

- Look out for microaggressions (or worse) during an event, and take action when you spot them.

6

HIRING PRACTICES

The hiring pipeline is an easy scapegoat. You've probably heard the excuses. Maybe you've even made some of them yourself. I know I have.

"There aren't enough female candidates." "We don't get many people of color applying for jobs." "We'd hire them if we could find them."

The list goes on.

Yet people who are members of these underrepresented groups are often bewildered. Many eager and qualified candidates, working hard to get hired, are passed over. They feel unnoticed. Invisible even.

And it's more than anecdotal. The tech industry in particular has a quantifiable problem compared to other industries that employ software engineers. In 2015, LinkedIn measured gender equality across industries and discovered something interesting. Roughly one-third of software engineers employed in health care, government, education, and nonprofits were women, compared to a dinky one-fifth in tech itself.[51]

Some might say there's "a higher bar" in tech than in other industries, and that tech companies don't want to "lower the bar" to hire members of underrepresented groups. This is just another excuse, and a bigoted one at that. Joelle Emerson, founder of diversity and inclusion consultancy organization Paradigm, writes:

> *The concern about "lowering the bar" stems from an incorrect (and biased) belief that a company has a high bar designed to hire the best people, and the reason it hasn't hired more diverse people is that they aren't able to meet that bar. In fact, in many cases it's the opposite: companies have a poorly designed hiring bar that fails to adequately evaluate highly qualified, and often diverse, candidates.*[52]

I've experienced this poorly designed hiring bar firsthand. Early in my career, I interviewed for a software engineering job on the same day and at the same company as my partner Tim. At that point, our resumes were almost identical. We'd graduated with computer science degrees from the same university. When we first entered the workforce, we'd worked at a research institute on the same project. We'd even published a technical paper together.

When Tim and I decided to move to Silicon Valley, we applied for jobs at many of the same companies, which was not surprising, given our common interests and experience.

What *was* surprising was what happened during one long day of interviews.

A large tech company brought us onsite to interview for software development roles. In side-by-side conference rooms, my partner and I talked with each person on the interview team. After someone interviewed Tim, they came to interview me, and vice versa. It went on for hours. In our rental car on the way back to our hotel, we compared notes.

And that's when I discovered the unconscious bias that had been in play.

As Tim shared the tough questions he'd been asked, I was shocked. By contrast, my interviews were superficial and skirted any difficult technical topics. I couldn't believe the difference. In the few seconds it took the interviewers to close the door to the room my husband was in, take a few steps, and open the door to the room I was in, they lowered the bar. And they did so before I'd said a word on my own behalf.

Turns out, we both got job offers from that company. But there was no way I was joining a team that viewed me as a woman who lacked the same technical chops as a man. I declined, and I never looked back. I joined a different company and went on to build my career at places that valued my skills and talents regardless of my gender.

In addition to lowering the bar, companies find other ways to bungle the hiring process. Alison Wynn, a postdoctoral fellow at Stanford University's Clayman Institute for Gender Research, and Stanford sociology professor Shelley Correll studied on-campus recruiting sessions for graduating STEM students, and found that many companies alienated women from the moment they walked in the door.[53] Instead of focusing on compelling work and advancement opportunities, the mostly male recruiters and engineers spoke about their companies' frat-like cultures, free food, dry cleaning, and other perks (many of which underscored the expectation that employees spend most of their life at the office). Their presentations included sexist jokes and imagery. Speakers often made comments that disparaged women or depicted them as sexualized objects instead of technical colleagues.

Makinde Adeagbo, a software engineer who has worked at Pinterest, Dropbox, and Facebook, shared this story of an appalling interview experience he had to endure:

*The technical founder/CEO walked into the room to ask a few technical questions. He was the author of a large, open source project. So, while I'd never met him before, I recognized his name and expected a challenging interview. Shockingly, his first question had nothing to do with technology. "Why do all the Black kids sit at the same table at school?" he asked. I was taken aback but tried to explain the social dynamics that might be at play. He followed with, "Why is it no longer okay to say n****r?" [I'd] never had that cutting word said to me and had a serious choice to make. Should I stand up and leave, or treat this as a teaching moment? It took mettle, but I chose the latter and gave the best 3 minute summary of 20th-century race relations that I could come up with. I finished the interview loop and went back to campus. When the recruiter called and congratulated me on getting an offer, I immediately declined, citing "severe cultural differences."* [54]

The rest of this chapter explores ideas for treating candidates equitably and strategies for hiring a more diverse workforce. Sure, there are some automated tools to help remove or mitigate bias during the hiring process, but they are not (yet) comprehensive. Instead of exploring the automated options, I will share everyday actions for anyone involved in the hiring process.

Specifically, I'll share approaches I've used in consulting projects for companies who want to attract and hire underrepresented candidates. For these projects, I often use this checklist from the National Center for Women in Information Technology, slightly modified to include other underrepresented groups and non-tech fields:[55]

- Do you use language and images to convey that people from marginalized groups belong at your workplace?
- Do you emphasize an inclusive work culture?

- Do you showcase how your company's work is contributing to social good? The social value of work can attract candidates from marginalized groups.

While most clients I've worked with tend to do well in these three areas, there is always something for them to improve. And some of those areas for improvement are more surprising than others.

Creating a great careers web page

A company's careers page is one of the first places a potential employee will visit to learn more about the company's culture, working environment, and advancement opportunities. If your company is serious about attracting a diverse pool of candidates, make sure this page is welcoming to them.

Use diverse images and inclusive language

First, look at the photos on your company's careers page. Do the photos show people of all kinds thriving at the company? Or are they full of young white dudes having a good time? Here are some issues that I've flagged for past clients:

- A photo of a dozen people dressed in camouflage overalls and carrying paintball rifles. Ten men and one woman were standing and smiling. Another woman was sitting on the ground, not looking happy at all.
- One company had a nice rotation of photos showing employees in different settings, yet the website always displayed the same one first: two white male cyclists wearing jerseys with the company logo. Why not lead with a photo showing more diversity?
- A photo of employees enjoying a dance party, in what looked like a mosh pit. One man was on his back, held

up by the others who jostled him around the pit. The red flag? As a woman, I couldn't imagine having others' hands all over my body, potentially even groping me. If this was how the company had fun, count me out.

Imagine how a woman, a person of color, or a disabled person would feel seeing these images before submitting their resume. They'd see people who look nothing like them engaging in activities that don't appeal to them and broadcasting an uninviting culture. Candidates need to be able to envision themselves working at a company before they feel comfortable applying, and reflecting their own experience through photos is a crucial way to do that. (I touched on this practice in Chapter 5, because the imagery used to promote events also needs to be diverse and inclusive.)

In addition, while photos are important, don't forget about the power of language.

In describing their organizational culture, one of my clients, a small start-up, emphasized the importance of their after-hour LAN parties. I have to admit I didn't know what a LAN party was, so I searched online and discovered that it's when a local area network (LAN) is used to connect people playing multiplayer video games. At the time, the Entertainment Software Association reported that about half of all computer/video gamers were women, but this ratio dropped to around 15 percent with massive multiplayer games.[56] This company might have been unintentionally eliminating female candidates by nurturing this aspect of their culture and emphasizing it on their careers page.

While you shouldn't hide important aspects of your company's culture, be sure to highlight things that show a commitment to creating an inclusive workplace. For example, if you offer resource groups for underrepresented groups, be loud and proud about them.

I especially appreciate the inclusive way Change.org described what they look for in candidates:

- Your coworkers are high-impact, low-ego, and have a deep respect for our members. We expect you to be the same.

- All qualified applicants will receive consideration for employment without regard to race, colour, national origin, religion, sexual orientation, gender, gender identity, age, physical disability, or length of time spent unemployed.[57]

If your company contributes to social good, say so

As the National Center for Women in Information Technology points out, the social value of work can attract candidates from marginalized groups. If your company is mission-led, with a goal of being economically successful while also having a positive impact on society, be sure this is emphasized on the careers page.

Alternatively, if your company doesn't have such a mission, look for ways to appeal to candidates who want to contribute to social good. Does your organization offer volunteering opportunities? Do you have customers who utilize your product offerings for their own mission-driven strategic goals? I remember speaking with a company that launches satellites to collect data from space. As I asked about their customers, I heard inspiring stories. One utilized weather data to improve farming yields. Another relied on maritime traffic data to go after pirates. If you can, showcase how your customers are making a positive impact in the world.

Emphasize employee benefits

Last but not least, review the language used to describe employee benefits on your company's careers page. Specifically, are you highlighting parental and family leave benefits? While applicable to all, these benefits are especially important to women, who are the primary caregivers in our society.[58]

Whether through photos, the language used to describe your company's culture and social impact, employee benefits, or other means, members of marginalized groups will evaluate your company by how it's represented on the careers page. Think about the messages you want to send, and ensure that this page reinforces them.

Crafting equity-focused job descriptions

Let's move on to job descriptions themselves, and the role they play in attracting a diverse candidate pool. Once again, I recommend starting with a checklist created by the National Center for Women and Information Technology:

- Are all of the criteria listed necessary for doing this job well?
- Do any of the criteria reflect typical assumptions about the "kind of person" you think usually does this job? If so, ask whether these are truly necessary for the job or whether they reflect subtle biases about who traditionally does this job.
- Do you provide a way to account for important life experiences that may not show up on traditional resumes but that can indicate likelihood for success in this job?
- Does the language in the description or advertisement subtly reflect gender or racial stereotypes/preferences

(e.g., language such as "high-powered," "results-driven," "action-oriented," "people person")?

- Do you include and value criteria such as "ability to work on a diverse team or with a diverse range of people"?[59]

This list is a great starting point for any allies charged with writing job descriptions or ads. Let's dive into some concrete examples that put them into action.

Avoid biased language

This may seem obvious and straightforward, yet biased language can easily creep into job postings, such as "guy," "craftsman," "he/him/his," and "right-hand man." And there's other language to be aware of. Using masculine-coded words like "aggressive," "competitive," and "individual" can deter women from applying.[60] Change this language in order to be welcoming to a wider candidate pool. You can use an automated online tool to do this, or get help from a keen-eyed editor.

To show you what this might look like, here's a job description from the "Tech Companies That Only Hire Men" Tumblr account, edited to be less biased:[61]

Before	After
Entrepreneurial Minded Small Business seeks "Fireman" Operations Associate	Entrepreneurial Minded Small Business seeks Operations Associate
Aggressive, assertive, "get stuff done"/"take charge" type personality sought for a position of operations manager and assistant to Chief Operating Officer of dot com technology company.	Organized, motivated individual sought for a position of operations manager and assistant to Chief Operating Officer of dot com technology company.

Limit the number of requirements to five

You've probably heard about a now-famous internal Hewlett-Packard study that found that women applied for a promotion only when they believed they met 100 percent of the qualifications listed for the job, while men applied when they thought they could meet 60 percent of the job requirements.[62]

HP's findings have been validated by other research. In *How to Lead*, Jo Owen describes how men applied for head teaching roles when they thought they were 50 percent ready, while women wanted to be nearer to 100 percent ready before taking on the responsibility.[63] Leadership development trainer Tara Mohr dug deeper and found that the problem isn't a lack of confidence in women applicants. She polled more than a thousand men and women and found that both genders were likely to avoid applying for jobs if they believed they didn't meet the qualifications. In an article for *Harvard Business Review*, Tara writes:

> *They didn't see the hiring process as one where advocacy, relationships, or a creative approach to framing one's expertise could overcome not having the skills and experiences outlined in the job qualifications. What held them back from applying was not a mistaken perception about themselves, but a mistaken perception about the hiring process.*[64]

Given this research, review job descriptions your company plans to post and remove any requirements that aren't truly necessary for the roles they describe. In fact, I recommend shooting for five at most. While it's not a magic number, it does set an aspirational goal for minimizing job requirements.

Apply this same rule to the number of years of experience required in particular skills. Ask yourself: If a strong candidate came along with only two years working with Java, would you hire them even if your job posting says you require three to five years? If your answer is yes, you shouldn't list a required number of years at all. Likewise, cut the "nice to have" and "preferred" requirements unless you truly need this experience (in which case, call them out as "full" requirements).

Here's an example from one of my clients of what this can look like. This posting is for an automation engineer role:

Before	After
4-6 years experience in hands-on Quality Assurance testing and release of multi-tier applications with multiple browsers (IE, Firefox, Mozilla, Safari, Netscape) and platforms (Windows, Linux)	Experience in hands-on Quality Assurance testing and release of multi-tier applications with multiple browsers and multiple platforms
Expert level load testing and stress testing skills in a web 2.0 environment	Experience leading web application test projects from planning to release
Deep knowledge of automation tools and frameworks	Load testing and stress testing skills in a web 2.0 environment
Proficient in programming and scripting using Python, Selenium	Experience with Python, Selenium, SQL, automation tools and automation frameworks
Experience leading web application test projects from planning to release	
Expert understanding of QA methodology and the software development lifecycle	
Ability to develop a clear and concise testing strategy and craft robust, comprehensive test plans to verify functionality	
Experience with automated tests	
Ability to work in an exciting environment and meet bold deadlines	
Excellent organization and interpersonal skills	
Working knowledge of SQL	
Strong verbal and written communication skills	
Motivated and assertive in learning and owning projects	
BS or equivalent experience in Computer Science or related Engineering field preferred	

With a simpler set of requirements, you should attract more women, who might otherwise not apply if they don't meet every single requirement on the list, as well as people with unconventional educational backgrounds and other diverse experiences.

If you feel like paring down job postings is "lowering the bar," check yourself. What we're doing here is editing writing that's often bloated and needlessly intimidating. Removing "preferred" items doesn't open a company up to a flood of unqualified candidates; rather, it forces the company to present a clearer picture of what it needs from the person who'll fill this role.

Don't include requirements unless they are truly required

I've written my fair share of job descriptions, and I bet that all of them listed "bachelor's degree or higher" as a requirement. It was a convention to attract a certain caliber of talent. Yet, in reality, the skills needed to perform many of these jobs could have just as easily been gained via life experience or some nontraditional education.

In certain tech circles, contributing to open source projects is a badge of honor because it involves writing code that others can use for free and build upon. People who spend free time coding are sometimes seen as more "serious" engineers. When hiring software engineers, it can be tempting to look for people with open source experience because of the credibility that comes along with it. Yet 95 percent of open source contributors are men.[65] The landscape can be harsh—with a lack of role models for women and nonbinary individuals, competing personal and family priorities, a combative hacker ethic, "flame wars," and the difficulty women face when receiving adequate recognition for contributions. Understandably, many women choose not to participate.

If a certain degree or open source experience is a strict requirement for a position, then of course it should be listed as a requirement in the job description. Otherwise, don't mention it.

Before	After
3-5 years open source experience preferred	

Consider whether you really need to evaluate candidates' GitHub profiles

Some job sites ask technical candidates for their GitHub profiles. Recruiters and hiring managers can then explore the candidates' source code firsthand to evaluate the code they've published, the projects they've forked, and the commits they've landed. Sounds good on the surface, but here's the rub: It assumes candidates are writing code in their free time (and aren't busy working a second job to pay the bills, handling childcare responsibilities, or balancing other demands on their time). It's basically another sign of privilege, not technical prowess.

So, before you ask to see someone's GitHub activity, ask yourself if you truly need to.

For managerial positions, seek experience with diverse teams

If you're hiring a manager or a team lead, do you want to attract candidates who care about diversity, some of whom may be from underrepresented groups themselves? Consider including "experience hiring and leading diverse teams" as a requirement. Send a clear message that this experience is both relevant and desired.

Before	After
Ability to influence people across the organization	Ability to influence people across the organization
Ability to coach your reports to grow a high-performance team	Ability to coach your reports to grow a high-performance team
	Experience hiring and leading diverse teams

Attracting candidates from underrepresented groups

Now, let's move on to some ideas for diversifying candidate pools. Experienced applicants from marginalized groups are out there, and attracting them to your company is not the impossible task that pipeline-blamers think it is.

Vary where you post your openings

As a female CEO, Kendall Tucker thought it would be easy to find strong female candidates for openings at her company, Polis. But she was receiving 95 percent male applicants for all job postings.

To diversify her team, she employed a number of strategies. While much of what she did was familiar territory for me, she did point out one approach I hadn't thought of before: "Post on a variety of job sites to get a diverse candidate pool."

It turns out that for positions at Polis, job postings on LinkedIn attracted up to 90 percent male engineering applicants, where Angellist, Indeed, Glassdoor, and Google attracted more balanced candidate pools.[66] Depending on your company, location, and the position you're posting, you may attract a diversity of applicants through LinkedIn. But why not cast a wider net?

Tap your current workforce

Ask employees to recommend people from under-represented groups who they've worked with before. Encourage them to dig deep into their networks if they have to. Hold sourcing parties to focus on underrepresented demographics. Offer a referral bonus for these candidates, or a larger amount if you have a referral bonus program already in place. It might encourage people to dig even deeper into their networks.

Pinterest employed this tactic and saw amazing results. Instead of just asking for "referrals"—which, as we discussed in Chapter 4, tend to be drawn from people's naturally homogeneous networks—the company requested engineering referrals for women and candidates from underrepresented ethnic backgrounds specifically. These referrals were requested during a six-week "challenge" period, a device for adding excitement and making the entire employee base feel invested in increasing diversity. During those six weeks, Pinterest saw a 24 percent increase in the number of women referred and 55 times as many candidates from underrepresented ethnic backgrounds.[67]

Create inclusive hiring policies

In 2002, the National Football League instituted the Rooney Rule, which states that all teams are required to interview at least one candidate of color for all head coaching and senior football operation openings.[68] In 2016 film director J. J. Abrams created a hiring policy for his production company, Bad Robot, that required that women and people of color be considered for writing, directing, and acting jobs in a way that's proportional to their representation in the U.S. population.[69] Amazon and Microsoft have adopted similar tactics when hiring for open positions.[70] One of the best ways to ensure that candidates from under-represented groups actually get hired at your company is to craft a policy that makes finding and interviewing them mandatory.

Allies can put these practices into action both within their current companies and outside of them. The next time some-one asks, "Do you know anyone who'd be interested in [some cool opportunity]?" take a minute to think of people from underrepresented groups to recommend for the job.

Understand the journey

I know a college senior from East Los Angeles, a densely populated, working-class neighborhood. Maria is the first in her family to go to college, and she's studying computer science at an Ivy League school. Smart, driven, and imagina-tive, I'm proud to know her and excited to see where her career will take her.

Want to know how Maria spent her summers during college? Working at a children's day camp near her home.

She didn't pursue tech internships during the time she spent on campus either. When I asked Maria why, she said, "I didn't think I was qualified. Plus, I was too busy working my job at the school cafeteria to fit in interviews." That on-campus job was Maria's priority because she needed the income to make ends meet.

Does not having a tech internship make her less gifted as a programmer, or less able to grasp how to submit a pull request for a large code base? Of course not. But it *may* make her ever-so-slightly less appealing to recruiters on first glance.

When hiring recent college grads, many people make huge assumptions about students who haven't hit certain marks or pursued certain experiences, without ever asking why. Until you face a situation in which one of them says, "Well, I wanted to do those things, but here's why I couldn't," you might be unaware of this ingrained bias. Instead of excluding someone because they didn't have an internship at a name-brand company, work to understand their journey.

Best practices for interviewing

Bias can too easily creep into the interview process, like it did on that day my partner and I interviewed at the same company. And there's research showing the impact of bias. Resumes with African American–sounding names receive 50 percent fewer callbacks than resumes with white-sounding names. Candidates with accents, women, and working mothers are all rated less favorably than their peers.[71] Naturally, these biases lead to fewer hires of members of marginalized groups.

Then there's culture fit, and the age-old interview debrief question of, "Would you want to grab a beer with them?"

Back in the 1980s, culture fit and "chemistry" were all the rage. They sprang from the idea that if companies hired employees whose personalities and values aligned with organizational strategy, those employees would feel more invested in their jobs and become more loyal. Skills were important, but cultivating a workforce of like-minded people ran a close second. Over time, however, "culture fit" became code for something else: passing the friendship test. The whole "grab a beer" scenario prompted decision-makers to begin thinking of "culture fit" as relating to likeability, personal similarities, and chemistry with the interviewer. It gave them license to hire people they wanted to hang out with, and pass over people who might've been ideal for the job but clashed with their leadership styles.[72]

Fortunately, things are changing.

I remember attending a panel where Jeffrey Siminoff, who was then head of diversity at Twitter, made a truly memorable comment. "If I hear that a candidate isn't a culture fit, I ask if they could be a culture add." Right on.

In a similar vein, Aubrey Blanche, global head of diversity and belonging at Atlassian, recommends asking, "What will this candidate bring that we don't currently have on the team?"[73] Atlassian also has shifted its focus from "culture fit" to "values fit." It helps recruiters hire people who share the company's goals, but not necessarily the viewpoints or backgrounds of the interview team.[74]

Here are some ways to combat bias and avoid the "culture fit" trap:

- **Create objective criteria for reviewing resumes**. Choose the most critical requirements from the job description, and evaluate candidates on those qualities, not on their name, gender, age, favorite song, or other qualities that don't equate to being able to do the work.

- **Use structured interview tactics.** Create interview questions focused on the skills and abilities your company is seeking. Ask each interviewee the exact same questions in the exact same order. Create a standardized scale for evaluating candidates and rank every interviewee on the same scale.[75]

- **Consider asking candidates to perform a work test**, assigning them a task that's similar to what they'd do if hired. Work tests are among the most reliable predictors of how someone will do in a job.[76]

It's impossible to completely eliminate personal bias, but it's imperative to eliminate as much of it as possible. Especially for those who are truly committed to hiring workers from marginalized groups.

Want to better recognize your personal bias? Take a free, online implicit association test on Harvard's Project Implicit website.[77]

Evaluate potential new hires on their inclusion experience

If you're trying to build a more inclusive environment, "it makes sense to stop letting in folks who would work against that goal," says diversity and inclusion consultant Jason Wong.[78] This means screening for inclusive attitudes and experiences during the interview process.

One simple way to do this is to ask candidates, "How have you contributed to a diverse and inclusive environment?"

Pay attention to your interview team

Recently, my friend Paul told me about some positions that his company was trying to fill. The interview team was a cross-functional group who would work with the new hires. They'd already hired one person, who happened to be the same gender and race as the hiring manager herself—a woman of color. Now, they needed to hire one more. They'd interviewed many qualified candidates, all of whom happened to be Indian men. None were selected. Even though the interview team was using objective hiring criteria, Paul thought the team members might be biased against this demographic, and asked for my advice.

I recommended adopting an approach that Google followed for removing bias from performance calibration sessions. In his book *Work Rules*, Laszlo Bock describes how at the start of calibration meetings, everyone is given a simple handout describing common errors and biases that assessors make, and how to fix them.[79] Simply reminding managers of these biases was enough to eliminate many of them. So when you begin the hiring process at your own company, why not remind the team that bias can creep in? In addition, give team members actionable advice on how to mitigate it.

Here's another tip. When possible, make sure candidates meet at least one interviewer of their same gender or ethnicity. At Cisco, this practice resulted in a roughly 50 percent increase in the odds that a woman would be hired for a given position.[80]

Find the leaks

If it looks like your company is not netting enough applicants from underrepresented groups, find out why. Evaluate your process, identify where these candidates drop out, and iterate. Use metrics from HR or your recruiting team to understand where candidates from underrepresented backgrounds drop out during the hiring process. Is it during phone screens? Interviews? After the offer is made? Find out what's going wrong at which phase, and change that step.

For more ideas for being a better ally during the hiring process, check out the Leaky Tech Pipeline website from the Kapor Center for Social Impact.[81] The website's "Tech Workforce" section includes a "Featured Programs" subsection that connects the user to organizations that can help combat bias in interviewing, help companies find applicants from underrepresented groups, and shift workplace cultures.[82] Although it's a tech-specific site, many of the recommended tools can be used across industries.

Making offers and negotiating without bias

Imagine being in a situation where you have two equally qualified candidates and need to choose which to hire. My recommendation? Make the offer to the person who will most diversify your team, and then work hard to encourage them to say yes.

This course of action may seem obvious, but it doesn't always happen. Remember when Tim and I moved to Silicon Valley and were interviewing at the same companies? One of those companies called us one evening with an unusual request. The recruiter said that, while they wanted to hire both of us, recent budget cuts meant they had to cut back on their hiring. They had only one open position.

Then she asked a mind-boggling question: "Which one of you wants the offer?" I have to admit I was weirded out by this approach, and immediately decided I no longer wanted to work for them. I quickly handed the phone to Tim, summarized the conversation, and said, "Tell her you're interested, and she'll make you the offer." Which they did, and they lost out on hiring me, a female engineer who would have helped make their team more diverse.

Although my experience is likely unique, parallel situations arise more frequently. Hiring managers are often forced to choose between two equally qualified applicants and struggle to decide who should receive the offer. If the manager is truly dedicated to creating an inclusive team, they'll opt for the candidate who brings a new perspective due to race, class, sexuality, gender, ability, age, body size, religion, life experience, nationality, or some other characteristic.

One last thing

As you onboard new hires from underrepresented groups, consider that they might feel tokenized. They might believe that you hired them solely because you wanted a more diverse workforce, not because they were perfectly suited to the position. They might also be concerned that their new co-workers think the bar was lowered in order to make them an offer.

Here's a fantastic idea that Larissa Shapiro, a diversity and inclusion leader, shared with me:

> *Over our latest cohorts of interns, we have succeeded in massively changing the gender and ethnic diversity. And the students did seem to wonder if we had chosen them for their demographics, not their skills. I walked them through how we screen for interns, explaining how you only get through the (very) large initial pool by scoring well on our anonymized online code assessment, and that therefore the bar is no different for any of them. I explained how bias traditionally skews the selection process and how by blocking bias, we get the best talent, which is them. I could see the women and PoC [people of color] interns relax when we got through this. The screening is a firm and anonymized bar, and that helps.*[83]

Actions for Better Allies:
Strive to Hire Equitably

Allies can band together to banish the "leaky pipe-line" excuses and focus on employing strategies that are proven to attract diverse applicants. Here are some ways you can make this possible in your own company:

- Look at your company's careers web page and job descriptions. Remove biased language, weed out any requirements that aren't needed, and find ways to appeal to people from different backgrounds.

- During your next recruiting push, challenge current employees to refer members of underrepresented groups from their networks for open positions.

- Implement structured interviews for open positions.

7

MEETINGS IN THE WORKPLACE

Talk to a woman who works in an office, and she'll tell you about a time (or two or ten) when she felt frustrated, if not downright dejected, in a meeting. Perhaps she was asked to take notes or get coffee, even though those aren't her responsibilities. Perhaps she was talked over, or ignored. Perhaps someone claimed credit for the idea she had proposed earlier. Even in companies where codified policies are intentionally equitable, meeting culture can be almost comically biased.

I've seen this in action myself. Not too long ago, I sat on a fundraising committee for my alma mater. Our goal was to endow the computer science department's undergraduate teaching assistant program. During one of our calls, I suggested we approach a certain alum—a prominent venture capitalist. While he hadn't studied computer science, his investments could benefit from a larger pool of software engineers graduating from our university. I thought we might convince him to support our fundraising by pointing out how it would pay off for him down the road.

I raised this idea on the call, but it didn't go anywhere. Perhaps we had other contacts that seemed more promising at the time. Perhaps I wasn't convincing enough. Either way, we didn't pursue my suggestion.

Imagine my surprise when I received an email a few weeks later from a member of our committee asking me what I thought of approaching that same alum. After picking up my jaw from the floor, I quickly wrote back, "I think it's a great idea. That's why I suggested it a few weeks ago on our call."

To his credit, he replied, "I remembered that right after I sent the message. Sorry." If only every person in a leadership position were this self-aware.

Over the years, I've trained myself to call it out when a guy co-opts one of my ideas. However, other women and members of other marginalized groups may not feel comfortable being so bold, or may fear censure if they speak up for themselves. This, among other reasons, is why allies can and should be doing this.

Here's how to spot situations where you can take action, along with suggested actions to make meetings more balanced and equitable.

"Manterruptions"

In 2017, Fortune reported on a study that analyzed hearings of the U.S. Supreme Court over the past twelve years. The study found that women justices were interrupted three times more often than men, and that women initiated only four percent of the interruptions overall.[84]

Guess what: The same pattern appears across the tech industry and in the vast majority of corporate cultures. "Manterruptions" are a thing, and they're probably happening within your team.

There are a host of reasons why guys may be more comfortable or skilled at interrupting others. It may be that it's culturally acceptable. Or that men's vocal cords are longer, resulting in deeper voices that project well and help them break into conversations. Or it could be that women have been socialized to say, "Excuse me ..." or "May I ask ..." when beginning a thought, making it easier to be interrupted.

According to Deborah Tannen, a professor of linguistics at Georgetown University, women may also be easy targets for interruption because they are already fearful of appearing too talkative. In a 2017 *Time* article, she wrote:

> *One reason women tend to speak less at meetings, in my view, is that they don't want to come across as talking too much. It's a verbal analogue to taking up physical space. ... When they talk in a formal setting, many women try to take up less verbal space by being more succinct, speaking in a lower voice and speaking in a more tentative way. Women have good reason for such caution—what I've described as the double bind. If they talk in ways associated with authority, they can be seen as too aggressive, and subject to the damning labels so readily applied to them. But if they don't—if they hold back in these and other ways—they risk being underestimated.*[85]

She also pointed out that even when women are specifically asked to weigh in, they might get interrupted. For instance, at the 2017 World Science Festival, a lone woman panelist was ignored for a full hour before the male moderator asked for her input. When she started to speak, he almost immediately began speaking himself, giving his own interpretations of her theories.[86]

Regardless of the reasons—and regardless of the gender identity of the person being interrupted—allies have a role to play in creating inclusive meetings. When you work to minimize interruptions, you create a more equitable work-place, with the added bonus of helping everyone know that they're valued members of the team. Here are some everyday actions to take in your next meeting to help ensure that all voices are heard:

- When someone is interrupted, interject and say you'd like to hear them finish.
- If you see someone struggling to break into the conversation, say you'd like to hear other points of view.
- If you see a "repeat offender" who interrupts frequently, pull them aside and point it out.
- Nominate a "gatekeeper" to keep the conversations on track, perhaps using the "meeting role cards" from Frame Shift Consulting.[87]

"Bro-propriation" and idea hijacking

Let's say a person of color says something insightful or even game-changing in a meeting, only to have it dismissed or ignored. Then someone else says the same thing later and it's well received—or maybe even heralded. While the second person (often a white man) gets the kudos, the person who originally said it starts fuming inside.

This scenario is all too common, and the frustration is understandable. Allies can borrow a page from a group of women who figured out how to stop "bro-propriation" in its tracks.

In staff meetings during Barack Obama's first term as president, women adopted a strategy they called "amplification." When one of the female staffers made a key point, other women would repeat it and give credit to its author. This approach forced others in the room to recognize the contribution—and denied them the ability to claim it as their own.[88]

Women aren't the only ones who can amplify the voices of other women, and people of color aren't the only ones who can amplify the voices of other people of color. Anyone can do it for someone who is less likely to be heard. I try to do it myself in meetings I attend. Of course, there are times when I'm not quite on the ball, and I miss the opportunity to amplify an idea contributed by someone from an under-represented group. If someone else repeats it later in the meeting, I remind everyone who originated it, saying something like, "Great idea. Thanks to Jen for surfacing it earlier."

And that's not all. I strive to give people credit for saying the same brilliant idea, even if they did so in a previous meeting. Here's what that might look like: "I like that idea a lot. In fact, when Ana brought that up last week in our one-on-one, I learned the following ..."

Not only do I want to amplify Ana's idea, I also hope to show her respect and help her build credibility by saying that I learned from her.

Another way to combat idea hijacking? Give credit to the project owner, even if they aren't in the room. Here's a good reminder of the simple, yet important, action of acknowledging someone's work, even (or especially) if they aren't present. Molly Peeples, an astronomer, recently tweeted:[89]

Molly Peeples @astronomolly · Jul 18
Meeting scene this morning:
Person: "& [Senior Man who isn't in the room]'s project ..."
Senior White Male: "No, that is [Junior Woman who also isn't in the room]'s initiative; she did all the hard work; call it [Woman's Last Name]'s project".

This is how you do it, people.

💬 21   🔁 552   ♡ 3.3K   ✉

Allies can use their positions of privilege to stop idea hijacking in its tracks. Let's amplify and showcase the ideas coming from the marginalized people all around us. Let's make this happen.

Off-topic questions and showboating

In August 2018, the *Washington Post* wrote about how conservative commentator Ben Shapiro challenged New York congressional candidate Alexandria Ocasio-Cortez to a debate, offering to donate $10,000 to her campaign or a charity of choice if she accepted.[90] Ben was not running for office at all—much less as an opponent to Alexandria —and his offer of payment would likely have been a campaign violation. This was not an offer made in good faith, this was showboating. After attempting to ignore the gambit for a day or so, Alexandria responded via Twitter, saying: "Just like catcalling, I don't owe a response to unsolicited requests from men with bad intentions. And also like catcalling, for some reason they feel entitled to one."

In presentations during meetings, a similar phenomenon can happen. People might ask off-topic questions to test presenters, undermine their credibility, and make themselves look smart in the process. It's a power play that's been used for years and can be incredibly distracting, forcing someone who was in a position of authority at the beginning of the meeting to suddenly have to defend their expertise.

Just like Representative Alexandria Ocasio-Cortez pointed out, women don't owe a response to off-topic requests from men (or anyone else). Marginalized people shouldn't have to defend themselves when disruptors feel the need to question their credentials. Allies can be on the lookout for these kinds of questions and shut them down.

Want an example of how an ally handled showboating beautifully? Hilary J. Scarsella—an expert in trauma, theology, and religious practice—told her Facebook audience about an experience she had at an airport after speaking at a conference. In a nutshell, she was sitting next to another speaker from the conference, and a man sitting across from them started a conversation. When he heard about the conference they'd spoken at, he launched into a diatribe about her area of expertise.

And then an epic and inspiring thing happened. As the man stood up to catch his plane, the other speaker leaned over and said, "Dude, you missed an opportunity. You had an expert in theology and trauma sitting in front of you. You say you're interested in these things but you didn't ask her a single question. You didn't try to learn anything at all from her." The speaker continued: "You know she has advanced degrees and is published but you just tried to show her that you know more about her work than she does. You missed out. Big fail, man."[91]

Well played.

Meeting housework

Meetings generate office housework. From taking minutes to scheduling follow-ups to clearing coffee cups from the table before leaving the room, there are always a bunch of administrative tasks that need to get done. Women tend to absorb these tasks, either because they're asked to or because they simply roll up their sleeves and get the job done.

You can avoid this pattern by making office housework tasks rotating responsibilities for your regular meetings. Set up a schedule for taking minutes, clearing the table, and so forth. For one-off meetings, consider asking only men to do these tasks, in order to send a strong disrupt-the-status-quo message: "Hey Mark—could you bring the leftover pizza over to the kitchen on your way out? And stick a note on them that they're up for grabs."

(Much, much more on this in Chapter 8.)

Misdirected questions

A few years back, Geraldine Mongold was working as an IT project manager at a construction company. In meetings, she was usually the only woman in the room, and the guys around the table would direct their questions to Andy, her key stakeholder. Recognizing this pattern, Andy always stepped back and said, "Geraldine is the project manager, I'm just the procurement guy."

In a similar vein, information security leader Chad Loder recalls attending customer meetings with one of his employees, Susan, a sales engineer who could answer detailed technical questions about their company's product. All too often, customers would direct all of their questions to him, not Susan. He would say, "Well, Susan wrote the API for this," and turn the conversation over to her.

Geraldine and Susan are not alone. In the 2017 "Elephant in the Valley" survey, more than two hundred women working in tech positions were polled.[92] Of women with at least ten years of experience working in tech, 84 percent said they had seen a question directed toward a male colleague when they themselves were the most qualified person in the meeting to answer it. And it's not just men who are guilty of this, because people of all gender identities are taught to assume that men naturally hold more power.

This trend also isn't limited to tech. I heard the following from Elizabeth Giorgi, founder and CEO of video production company Mighteor:

> *Over the years, one of the most common things that happens is when we are meeting with a new client, they will often assume one of my male colleagues is the founder. I have been so fortunate that the men of character I work with have often quickly clarified. However, I am also fervent in clearing it up myself. There are many subtle ways to do this. My favorite is to wait until the conversation starts to flow and saying something simple like, "When I founded this company ..." or "As the owner of this organization ..." These statements show confidence, they clarify the question at hand, and they provide an opportunity to educate without shaming.*[93]

Chances are good that misdirected questions surface in meetings at your company, too. As an ally, redirect the question to the most qualified person. All it takes is a simple "Deepa is the expert on that topic. Let's hear from her" or "Elizabeth is our founder. She's the best person to answer your question."

Economy seating

If you observe coworkers in meetings, you'll likely notice white men sitting in the center seats around the table. Members of underrepresented groups, by contrast, often gravitate toward the ends of the table and the edges of the room, away from positions that convey status. In other words, they take seats in the economy section.

Allies can invite marginalized people to take the power seats. In fact, allies can go even further and offer to swap seats with them. Here's how: "Sarah, I know you're going to make some killer points today. Why don't you take my seat so everyone can hear you better." Or, make some room at the table and say, "Asif, would you sit by me today? This is really the best seat in the house."

Enlisting a buddy

Many meetings have back channels, with key players suggesting changes to tactics and strategies in the moment via direct messaging or texting. Why not leverage the back channel to up your ally skills? Ask a trusted peer to message you when you could be a better ally, and offer to do the same for them.

Nithya Ruff, who leads the open source office at Comcast and is also on the board of the Linux Foundation, has just such a relationship with a male colleague. She messages him when she thinks he could be a better supporter of herself or other women in the room. Similarly he alerts her if there are things she should pay attention to in Twitter conversations.

She also sees the power in women being back channel buddies for each other, to perform sanity checks on meeting dynamics. "Am I reading this correctly?" or "Am I over-reacting?"

Wondering how you might nudge your own colleagues and allies through a direct message or text? Here's what it might look like:

- "Dude, you forgot to give Miriam a shout-out in your project update."
- "Hey, Jasmin made the same point you just made earlier in the meeting. Give her credit."
- "Stop talking. It's time to listen."

One last thing

I can't believe I have to write this, but in the interest of covering all bases I will. Don't take your team to a lunch meeting at a strip club, even if it has a $5 all-you-can-eat buffet. Not everyone is going to feel comfortable going, and they may miss out on key discussions if they don't attend. Unless your company literally is a strip club, don't bring job candidates there, or close business deals there either.

You may even need to revise your travel and entertainment policy to reflect your company's values. These policies can be subtle tools for creating more inclusive environments. A start-up founder once told with me that he had to clarify in his T&E policy that strip club charges were not allowable expenses. He did so after reviewing an expense report for three of his salespeople, who had divided a $1,500 tab from bringing customers to a strip club. You know what else? He declined to cover those expenses.

As you organize or are invited to out-of-the-office meetings, make sure the locales are places where everyone will feel comfortable and welcome. And consider reviewing your company's policies to identify how they could better reinforce a culture of inclusive outings.

Actions for Better Allies:
Amplify and Advocate in Meetings

At many companies, much of the workday is spent in meetings. This means that ensuring the voices of members of underrepresented groups are heard and valued is essential to creating an inclusive work culture.

- Challenge yourself to notice and take action when interruptions happen in meetings.

- Cultivate a culture of credit: Encourage everyone around you to acknowledge the originator of ideas as often as possible.

- Be vigilant and push back on off-topic questions and showboating.

- Take note of how attendees arrange themselves in meeting rooms. Do what you can to mix up seating arrangements so your marginalized coworkers are in power positions.

- Ask a back channel buddy to keep you accountable.

8

OFFICE HOUSEWORK

In the summer of 2017, a tech company hired me to advise and coach the steering committee for their women's employee resource group. I remember attending one of their monthly meetings, which started with the chairperson reviewing a file on her laptop to figure out whose turn it was to take notes. (Turns out that at the beginning of the year, they had made a rotation schedule for note-taking and a few other administrative tasks.) When she announced that it was Bob's turn, the only male member of the committee announced, "I'm not really very good at taking notes, so someone else should do that."

I was taken aback, but not so much that I didn't think of something to say in the moment. In fact, I believe I had a spot-on response: "Practice makes perfect, and this is the perfect place to practice." There was no way I was going to let Bob get away with not doing his fair share of the meeting housework. Especially given the research on the topic.

What research, you ask? After Ellen Pao lost her gender discrimination lawsuit against Kleiner Perkins in 2015, a group of women decided to run a survey. They realized that while many women had similar stories to Ellen's, most men were surprised and unaware of the issues facing women in the workplace. They decided to collect data as proof that discrimination happens across tech. After surveying hundreds of women with at least ten years of work experience, most of it in Silicon Valley, they published the results. Their report is called "The Elephant in the Valley." I mentioned it briefly in the previous chapter, and it's pretty telling.

One piece of data that surfaced in the final report: Almost half of the women surveyed (47 percent) had been asked to perform lower-level tasks that male colleagues were not asked to do. In other words, they'd been asked to take on more office housework.[94]

Another research study found that women tend to volunteer for these "non-promotable" tasks more than men; that women are more frequently asked to take such tasks on; and that when asked, they are more likely to say yes.[95] And research from the Center for WorkLife Law at the University of California, Hastings College of the Law, indicates that women of color are tasked with office housework even more frequently than their white colleagues.[96] This imbalance means that people who are saddled with food ordering, room cleanup, and other administrative duties that are not part of their job description may miss out on more visible, notable tasks and eventually be conceptualized as lower-level employees, even if they have high potential. Allies can change this dynamic. In fact, it's the responsibility of allies to change it.

Understanding office housework

Every workplace has office housework—tasks that need to get done but don't impact the bottom line. Chances are they don't lead to career growth; they may even impact it negatively. The most obvious example of office housework is taking the minutes at a meeting if that's not part of one's job description. (As a former program manager and epic note-taker, I know the value of good notes. I'm not diminishing this role at all. I'm simply calling it out as office housework if it's not part of a person's assigned responsibilities.)

There are many more examples. In fact, each time I coach women on how to rise above office housework, I learn about more ways it shows up. Here are some administrative and undervalued tasks that my female clients have been asked to do that they don't see their male peers being tapped for:

- Schedule the follow-up meeting
- Order food or make reservations at a restaurant
- Clean whiteboards and clear coffee mugs at the end of a meeting
- Plan a team-building event
- Join the hiring committee for another team
- Collect money and purchase a gift for a teammate's new baby
- Be the only mentor for the interns, every summer

If women accept these tasks when asked, they may be kept from their real work. If they refuse, they may be pegged as selfish or touchy. This issue is compounded for women of color. Caty, a manager at a technology company, told *Harvard Business Review*, "As a visibly black woman in the workplace, I am often caught in a double-bind where if I don't accept the office housework, I'm considered an 'Angry Black' woman."[97]

Women are also often perceived as "enjoying" this work simply because they are more likely to do it. Recently, I taught a workshop at a software engineering school in San Francisco. The topic was how to be a better ally, and during the segment on office housework, one of the men in attendance asked, "But what if someone enjoys doing these tasks? Like Julie, who frequently washes mugs that are left in the sink? I think she enjoys cleaning up because it helps her handle stress." I then asked if Julie was also in the workshop. She was. And was it true that she enjoyed washing the mugs? She vehemently answered "No." She did this task only because she hated seeing a sink full of mugs a lot more than she minded washing them.

Organizing baby showers for teammates or mentoring new employees may or may not be enjoyable for the person who takes on these responsibilities. It doesn't actually matter. Regardless of whether someone enjoys doing these tasks or not, there can be a negative impact. An impact on how they are perceived. An impact on the work they need to deliver. An impact on their career.

The impact of office housework

Back in 2015 Richard Branson, founder of the Virgin Group, stepped forward to champion spreading office housework across staff of all genders. In particular, he wanted companies to stop assigning note-taking duties exclusively to women. In a company blog post, he wrote:

> *Not only is this unfair to women, but it's also disadvantageous to men. It's time for men to step up and do their share of support work. On top of counteracting gender bias in the workforce, it will also give men a better understanding of what*

[sic] going on within the business and what needs to be done to make things run more effectively.[98]

He also pointed out that while note-taking is informative, it is viewed as menial work. "In my experience, 99 percent of people in leadership roles don't take notes," he wrote, and I agree.[99] C-level executives don't take meeting minutes and regional directors don't order team lunches. When we take on office housework, we move into a subservient role, which can lead to being seen as less valuable than our peers. When we volunteer to take notes or wash mugs, we look less leaderly in a culture that devalues these tasks.

By spending time on housework tasks, we have less time to spend on more valued projects. On contributions that directly impact the business. On deliverables that count during performance appraisals. On work that creates visibility and leads to career growth.

In some cases people from underrepresented groups are given work that's *adjacent* to visible or important assignments. For instance, a 2014 study of women lawyers found that 70 percent of those surveyed worked for firms where there were zero women—or just one token woman—sitting on powerful and influential compensation committees. The respondents also reported feeling that the committee work they *were* typically given—such as developing talent—did not do them any favors when annual reviews came around.[100] Different assignments might have bolstered their careers, but the ones they were handed simply dragged them down.

Office housework tasks can also interrupt flow. I heard from an engineer who loves babies and frequently offered to collect money to buy gifts for new parents on her team. Over time she started to regret it. Inevitably, she'd be hot on the trail of tracking down a gnarly coding bug when someone would stop by to chip in some money and sign the card, and stay for a few minutes to chat. It totally interrupted her flow, and she lost valuable time getting back to where she was.

Last but not least, those who are taking the meeting notes are often a step behind the conversation, documenting what has been said instead of making killer points themselves. By helping everyone else, they are putting themselves at a distinct disadvantage.

How to change office housework distribution

There are many ways allies can disrupt the norms around how office housework is handled. Depending on your position within a department or company, you can impact the distribution of this work using a variety of tactics:

- If you're part of a new committee or working group that's forming, recommend setting up a rotation schedule for any administrative tasks that aren't part of someone's job description. Think scheduling meetings, taking notes, timekeeping, and ordering food.

- If you're a supervisor, spread office housework tasks among your team. For example, if you notice one person is always tasked with mentoring the summer interns, say something like, "Ann's great at mentoring. But it's the perfect stretch assignment for Nick, who's never done it before."

- If you're a manager or mentor and notice someone regularly volunteering for menial tasks, talk to them in private. Let them know you're concerned that the office housework they're taking on will affect their career growth. Encourage them to look for more impactful tasks to get involved with, and offer a few examples to nudge them in the right direction.

Here are some phrases that your mentees or direct reports can use when people ask them to do office housework:

- **"I'll have to ask my manager about prioritizing it."** Unless the person making the request *is* the manager, it can be helpful to postpone agreeing to office housework until after discussing it with a supervisor or boss. Their input will provide cover for saying, "No."

- **"Why do you think I'm the right person to handle that?"** Forcing someone to articulate specific talents or credentials related to ordering lunch or scheduling a meeting often makes them realize their own bias.

- **"Remember, I volunteered last time. Let's spread the wealth."** The person making the request may need reminding that they should distribute office housework more evenly among team members.

Regardless of your position, as meetings break up, look around. If there are mugs, pastry boxes, or other post-meeting detritus left on the table, take a minute to throw out the trash and bring the rest to the nearest kitchen—especially if you're in a position of privilege or authority. Or point it out to someone walking out with you, and ask them to help out. If you don't, chances are the last woman to leave the room will feel compelled to clean up the mess.

If you have the ability to impact company policies, consider holding a meeting *about* office housework. You could facilitate a brainstorming session about which tasks qualify, discuss why it's detrimental to foist them on women and other marginalized employees, and identify approaches for disrupting how your team handles office housework.

There are many more ideas for effectively responding to unequitable requests in Ruchika Tulshyan's excellent article,

"Women of Color Get Asked to Do More 'Office House-work.' Here's How They Can Say No."[101] In preparation for your brainstorming session, consider circulating that article (and others on office housework) so attendees will have some background on the dynamics that will be discussed.

Relying on certain people or groups to handle tasks that don't drive business impact or lead to career growth is a prime example of unconscious bias. Most people who assume that women will do the office dishes don't even realize they're being chauvinistic until someone points it out. Allies can and should educate colleagues, helping to change how office housework is distributed and eradicating this erosive and harmful prejudice.

Actions for Better Allies:
Share the Load

Office housework isn't just aggravating. Calling exclusively on women, people of color, and members of other marginalized groups to perform it means preventing them from tackling more meaningful work. With that in mind:

- Share the work among the team. For example, if you notice one person is always tasked with mentoring the summer interns, say something like, "Ann's great at mentoring. But it's the perfect stretch assignment for Nick, who has never done it before."

- Set up a rotation for tasks like taking minutes or scheduling the next meeting.

- If you're in a position of privilege or authority, model better behavior yourself by clearing the lunch leftovers or used coffee mugs, rather than assuming someone else will take care of it.

- Never assume that certain coworkers are shouldering office housework because they "enjoy" it or find it "rewarding."

9

EVERYDAY LANGUAGE

Language is powerful, and, let's face it, shifts regularly to adapt to current events, trends, needs, and so forth. Words used in the past may no longer be the right ones to use today. They might go out of fashion, you might learn that they're noninclusive or harmful to others, or your own circumstances might change and affect what's appropriate or not. (For example, a parent decides to stop swearing to be a better role model for their child.)

Recently, I was talking about language with my son Ted, and he mentioned that "to orient oneself" has roots in aligning two maps eastward, toward the "Orient." Not too long ago, it was widely accepted practice to refer to Asia as "the Orient" and the people who lived there as "Orientals." Today, that's no longer the case. Our language shifted to use "Asia" and "Asians," which are more inclusive and respectful terms. (It's unlikely that anyone of Asian descent would take offense if you talk about "orientation," but the root of the word is still one that's decidedly outdated.)

Here's another example of how language changes over time in response to social shifts.

Brad Johnson, a professor at the U.S. Naval Academy and coauthor of *Athena Rising: How and Why Men Should Mentor Women,* told me he's seen many shifts away from inappropriate terms, especially because the ratio of women enrollees has doubled since he started teaching, from about 15 percent to about 30 percent. Years ago, Brad would hear his students using the term *WUBA*, pronounced "woobah." He didn't know what it meant until someone finally explained it to him: "Women with Unbelievably Big Asses," an incredibly demeaning and derogatory thing to say. He says that the term has all but vanished from common use—and that, in fact, if that word were to be used at the Naval Academy today, there would be a swift, negative response by other men.

Although many people accept that language is fluid and impacted by social forces, others resist change. It can be aggravating to discover that words or phrases that were acceptable for decades are suddenly taboo. But those who push back are often the ones with the most privilege, and the ones least likely to be insulted or harmed by the terms they refuse to give up. Those who resist change are also likely to have a narrow understanding of *why* a certain word or phrase is no longer acceptable. If they saw the big picture, they might not be so stubborn about removing it from their vocabularies.

So, this chapter looks at a wide variety of problematic terms and word categories that imply bias, cause harm, or otherwise generate negative responses in workplaces. Many are related to gender, identity, or ethnicity, but others touch on other traits or differences. Allies can help build more inclusive and welcoming workplaces by avoiding particular words and remaining open to future shifts in language. Allies can also apologize when they discover they've been unwittingly using a problematic term.

Speaking of which, this chapter is far from comprehensive. There are plenty of other words that are part of everyday language that are no longer acceptable—words that allies should be aware of to be more inclusive, especially in common workplace situations.

Being an ally is a journey, and part of that journey is being attuned to the ever-changing needs of those around us. That includes adjusting our everyday language. Let's explore a few terms and word groups that allies should avoid, and examine why they've fallen out of favor. I've curated this guidance from experts and other helpful sources, which are listed in the "Additional Resources" section later in this book.

Gendered language

Allies should always be on the lookout for unnecessarily gendered language. When it comes to modifying titles or roles, consider what value, if any, is added by including a gender term at all. Why say "female lawyer" when "lawyer" would do just fine? Why reinforce nursing as "women's work" by saying "male nurse" and implying that it's odd or unusual for a man to work in that field?

Allies working in male-dominated industries should be on the lookout for "man" terms that imply other genders aren't expected or welcome. I remember when it was common to estimate projects in terms of "man-hours"—and some people still do. Sure, there were more men working on these projects than women, but it was easy enough to start using the gender-neutral "work-hours" or, for software projects, "dev-hours."

Deb Liu, who has worked as vice president of marketplace at Facebook, believes that gendered language of all kinds can be harmful in the workplace. She writes:

> *Once I started documenting these words, I heard them every-where—in meetings, hallway conversations and presentations. Many of the masculine phrases like "manpower" and "right-hand man" were neutral to positive, usually indicating a position of strength while nearly all of the feminine ones, like "prima donna" and "Debbie downer" were negative and indicated weakness. These subtle sexist messages are all around us, and as a mother of a boy and two girls, I wonder what it says to them about the world we live in. If someone says a project is a "two-man job," who comes to mind for the opportunity? … The best way to confront unconscious bias is to force ourselves to be aware of how it is present all around us, even built directly into work lexicon we use every day.*[102]

Deb's story reminds me of something my daughter Emma experienced when studying computer science in college. One of her coding assignments included the encouraging note, "Man up and edit the stencil code. You can do it!" Once you start paying attention to "man" phrases, you'll notice how commonplace they are.

Because we live in a world where gender is a spectrum and professions aren't limited by gender, allies can do the most good by using and promoting gender-neutral terms. Be particularly mindful of the following examples.

Guys

Many people use the word *guys* to refer to a mixed-gender group. I have to admit I've done so a lot, both when talking to my family ("Hey guys, dinner is ready") and in professional settings ("Alright guys, let's wrap up this meeting.") And I can't even begin to count how many times I must have said "hey yous guys" as a kid, growing up in Rhode Island. (Fortunately, I broke myself of that habit a while ago.)

"But wait," you might be thinking, "*guys* is gender-neutral. After all, that's how everyone uses it. Plus it's been that way for years." You might even ask some female coworkers or friends and hear that they are perfectly fine with the term.

Well, it may be fine for many, but not for all. Imagine you're a woman or a nonbinary individual and need to use a restroom in a coffee shop. You find a door marked "guys." Would you go in, or would you look around for another option?

Or imagine you're a straight, cisgender man; how would you answer the question, "How many guys did you date in high school and college?"

Maybe "guys" isn't as gender-neutral as you thought.

I've been doing my best to stop using "guys" for a group that isn't all men. I want to be more inclusive of other genders, and I certainly don't want to give the impression that men are the preferred gender. Sure, it slips out every now and then, and when it does I'll say something like, "whoops, I meant to say 'folks.'" Or "friends" or "people" or "humans" or "y'all" or some other nongendered word. Want more options? Check out Kim Z. Dale's article "40 Gender-Neutral Alternatives to Saying 'You Guys,'" which includes great alternatives like "crew," "squad," and "cohort."[103]

Ladies and gentlemen

The age-old phrase, "Welcome, ladies and gentlemen," also needs a facelift. It's not inclusive of everyone in the room, because it fails to acknowledge people who are nonbinary. Even if you know that every person in the room is cisgender, there's no reason to adhere to exclusive language.

It's a good practice to always default to the most unbiased phrasing possible. So instead of "ladies and gentlemen," try using "distinguished guests" or a simple "good morning/ good afternoon everyone," like the London Tube announcers started using in 2017.[104]

Speaking of "ladies," that word can come across as patronizing for a number of reasons. Because "lady" is still related to nobility in some cultures, it can make modern women feel as though they're being reminded of a time when women were quieter, gentler, and more "well-behaved." The male equivalent is "gentleman," but aside from messages of welcome, this word has largely dropped from common usage. (Ever heard someone shout, "Hey, watch it, gentleman"? Me neither.) The derivative "ladylike" also hearkens back to less equitable times when women behaved in a certain demure way, and reinforces the false gender binary. Finally, "lady" has become a condescending prefix to jobs or activities that are associated with male culture: lady cop, lady umpire, lady politician.[105] Even though you may hear women calling each other "ladies" or even "gals" or "girls," I recommend allies say "women." It's more respectful.

Pronouns

For a long time, "he" was considered the default pronoun in the English language to refer to a single person. It took decades of effort for feminists to shift this standard by advocating for the use of "he or she" and "her or his," but many people still use "he" on occasion even if they don't know the gender of the person to whom they're referring. Doing so perpetuates bias. For example, imagine attending a hiring committee meeting for a software engineer position and hearing someone say, "When the candidate arrives, he should first meet with ___." The person is probably thinking about the mostly male job applicant pool for the role and reinforcing this stereotype by using the pronoun "he."

To circumvent this implicit gender bias and the awkwardness of saying "he or she," it's fine to use "them" and "they," even when talking about an individual person. The grammatically minded among us (including me) might find this awkward initially, but over time it becomes more familiar and natural. I'm now fine hearing (or saying), "When the candidate arrives, they should first meet with ___." In fact, I've even intentionally written this book using "they" and "them" in this way. (If your inner grammarian continues to resist, remember that revered writers including William Shakespeare and Jane Austen used "they" as a singular pronoun.[106])

In addition to employing "they" when a person's gender identity is uncertain, it's helpful to make yourself aware of the language someone uses to refer to themself. Many nonbinary people use "them" and "they." There are plenty of people, whether cisgender, trans, or nonbinary, for whom it is impossible to know what pronouns to use just by looking at them. Even some cisgender people forsake the traditional "he" or "she" pronouns for "they" or something else. It's presumptive to assign someone a pronoun based on their physical appearance.

Not sure what pronouns to use? As I learned from my friend Dom Brassey, introducing yourself with a simple "I use she and her. What pronouns do you use?" when meeting someone new is respectful, and their answer gives us clear guidance. If you don't want to ask, you can always just use "they" until you learn more.

Finally, please don't ask someone for their "preferred" pronouns. That makes it sound like using their pronouns is optional, which it's not.

Disability as a negative metaphor

Some of the most common and prominent problematic terms refer to gender or ethnicity, but there are important examples that disparage people who are disabled or have mental health conditions. This includes those whose conditions or disabilities may be invisible to the naked eye.

During a diversity and inclusion webinar I attended in 2018, one of the speakers surprised me with her less-than-inclusive language. Specifically, she used "nuts" and "crazy" to describe unusual business conditions. My concern? Using these terms in casual conversation can diminish the experience of people who live with mental health conditions. (It's similar to how I wouldn't use "retarded" as a synonym for "stupid" or "nonsensical.")

Instead of "crazy," here are some alternatives to consider: "unusual," "outrageous," "surprising," "wild," or even "unprecedented."

Along related lines, calling something "lame" when you find it to be subpar is disrespectful to people with physical disabilities. The term was coined hundreds of years ago to describe animals and people with injuries, but is now used to describe anything that isn't performing to standard.[107] This new, more liberal application implies that disabled people are themselves disappointing. Understandably, people with disabilities often object to having their collective identity used as the default proxy for virtually anything negative. Instead of "lame," try "mediocre," "unsatisfying," "meager," or terms I've used here, such as "subpar" or "disappointing."

There are many more examples of such linguistic microaggressions. In "Doing Social Justice: Thoughts on Ableist Language and Why It Matters," graduate student Rachel Cohen-Rottenberg wrote,

Disability metaphors abound in our culture, and they exist almost entirely as pejoratives. You see something wrong? Compare it to a disabled body or mind: Paralyzed. Lame. Crippled. Schizophrenic. Diseased. Sick. Want to launch an insult? The words are seemingly endless: Deaf. Dumb. Blind. Idiot. Moron. Imbecile. Crazy. Insane. Retard. Lunatic. Psycho. Spaz.[108]

To learn about alternatives to these metaphors, check out the comprehensive "Ableism/Language" list compiled by Lydia X. Z. Brown, chairperson of the Massachusetts Developmental Disabilities.[109]

Language that disrespects Indigenous peoples

Just the other day, I used the word "powwow" to refer to a group discussion I was about to facilitate. As the word came out of my mouth, I realized I should have chosen a different one. One that would be more inclusive and respectful of Native Americans and their heritage. Many nations still hold powwows to gather and celebrate, and none of them take place in corporate conference rooms.[110] Even if this weren't a term that was still in active use, it describes a specific type of event that honors a specific population, so appropriating it is insulting.

My friend Michelle Glauser—founder of Techtonica and creator of the Bay Area's 2015 #ILookLikeAnEngineer ad campaign—offers a slew of alternatives, including "meeting," "check-in," "talk," "huddle," and "one-on-one."[111] Right on.

There are plenty of other sayings that diminish or disparage the culture of Indigenous peoples. Examples include "going off the reservation," "lowest person on the totem pole," "too many chiefs, not enough Indians," and "Indian giver."[112] Let's stay away from all of them.

Back in Chapter 1, I told you about a white software engineer who, when asked to name her "spirit animal" as part of a team-building exercise, pushed back. She didn't want to take part in the cultural appropriation of Native American spiritual practices. Here's a nifty alternative I learned from Aubrey Blanche, global head of diversity and belonging at Atlassian: Use "patronus" instead.

Popular industry terms

During my twenty-five-year career working in tech, I know I've used many non-inclusive or outright harmful words and phrases, including "master/slave" to describe storage backup systems and "whitelist/blacklist" to filter items in algorithms. Despite their racist undertones, these terms are industry-standard and almost universally accepted. While it can be challenging to steer colleagues away from jargon and terms that have been widely used in their fields for decades, allies must focus on doing what's right instead of what's easy. And that includes eradicating insider language and shorthand terms that are problematic.

Here are a few more examples from various industries:

- Electrical components are often labeled as "male/female" parts. Why not use "pin/socket" or "plug/receptacle" instead?
- Many scientists and researchers use the term "blind" when referring to their research. Terms like "blind review" and "double-blind randomized controlled trial" are common. Why not say "masked" instead?
- In the publishing industry, a "dummy" describes an early layout mock-up with stand-in images. "Dummy" is also a slur for people who can't speak. Why not say "mock-up" instead?

Often changes in industry terms or company-specific words come from leadership. A few years ago, I attended a panel where Michael Lopp, then–vice president of engineering at Pinterest, mentioned his goal of using more inclusive language. In addition to steering clear of "guys" to refer to mixed-gender groups, he shared one other example. He'd started using "straw dog" as an alternative to "straw man" when talking about rough proposals. I'm betting the unexpected word choice caught people by surprise, and encouraged them to examine their language choices.

That said, changes can also come from collegial discussion. Security Nerdette launched a Twitter thread suggesting that programmers use "safelist/blocklist" instead of "whitelist/blacklist" and a fascinating discussion ensued. While some respondents insisted that the colors white and black were neutral in this context, others pointed out that the present-day effect (reinforcing unconscious racial bias) is more important than the origin (1600s and unrelated to race). Other tech experts chimed in with other ideas for term swaps, including replacing "master/slave" with "primary/replica." Many committed to making these changes in their own workplaces.[113]

To continue learning about using more inclusive language in your own workplace, consider making a "language matters" channel on your corporate Slack or other discussion tool. Health-care tech company Nuna has such a channel for co-workers to ask questions about non-inclusive language and suggest alternatives. The company also uses it to discuss effective ways to point out when someone uses problematic language and for staff to learn how to respond when called out for their own language choices.[114]

As your workplace identifies language you want to "retire," consider using a tool to automatically flag non-inclusive words and phrases and make alternate suggestions. I belong to a cross-company tech leadership Slack group with a Slackbot that looks for "guys," "crazy," "insane," "midget," "pimp," "has balls" and other such terms and replies automatically with an explanation of why the word or phrase isn't inclusive and some alternatives to consider. It's definitely effective. (In the "Additional Resources" section at the end of the book, you'll find an open source link you can use to create such a Slackbot for your company.)

Titles and honorifics

In 2018, across social media, women with PhDs started adding "Dr." to their profile names in order to claim their hard-earned achievement and to push back in solidarity against trolls who were calling them "arrogant," "immodest," or "vain" for doing so.

It all started with a tweet by Dr. Jensen Moore:[115]

Dr. Jensen Moore @MagicalPR · Jun 17

Added Dr. to my Twitter name today. Always felt I shouldn't because I'd been married to a "real" doctor (orthopedic surgeon). So I was just the "paper Dr." But I worked 3 jobs to put him through medical school WHILE getting my Ph.D. and having our 2 kids. So #ImmodestWomen it is.

628   2.3K   32K

Can you imagine a man getting flak for insisting that people use the right honorific when addressing him? Or calling him "vain" for referring to himself as Dr.? Recognizing this double standard, hundreds of women responded, many of them by adding Dr. to their own handles. I love that they used the #ImmodestWomen hashtag to draw attention to the issue. You know what else? I love that "Dr." is a gender-neutral title.

Let's support every person from a marginalized group who decides to be confident, authoritative, and proud of their hard-earned achievements—whether by claiming their credentials in their social media profiles or with some other action.

Unconscious demotions

In Chapters 4 and 5 I discussed the dangers of assuming someone holds a particular type of role based on their age, gender, or race. This type of inference is called an "unconscious demotion." In June 2018 psychology professor Marisa Franco tweeted:[116]

Marisa Franco @MarisaGFranco · Aug 14

Tip: Instead of asking unfamiliar faces in your department "are you a student?" ask "what is your role, here?" This helps folks who haven't traditionally been the face of academia-- young professors, professors of color, female professors in mostly male departments --belong.

254   8.6K   39K

In tech, this might look like someone asking, "Are you an intern?" or, "Do you work in marketing or HR?" (As before, while there's nothing wrong with those disciplines, this kind of assumption can be another signal to marginalized engineers that they don't belong.) On a movie set, this might look like someone asking "Are you a production assistant?" or "Can you get me a coffee, dear?"

To be more inclusive, follow Dr. Suzanne Wertheim's advice: Don't give an "unconscious demotion" by articulating that you think someone is in a position lower or less technical than their real position. Instead, ask an open-ended question.[117]

One last thing

Allies can play an important role by being role models for more inclusive language. At the Naval Academy, Brad Johnson told me that he believes internal language has shifted because senior leaders have made it a priority to use more inclusive language themselves. Also, there's an expectation that the men will police each other, because women are still the minority group. Sounds like a best practice for workplaces everywhere.

Actions for Better Allies:
Watch Your Words

As Security Nerdette pointed out in her Twitter thread, "How we spend our day is how we spend our life."[118] It may seem like word choice is a minor issue, but it's one that accumulates over time.

- Be aware and respectful of pronouns and gendered language. Lead by example in how you use (or don't use) both.

- Create a safe space for people in your workplace or industry to ask questions and discuss problematic language.

- Be aware that some terms you think are innocuous may be harmful to others. If you mess up, apologize.

PART THREE

ACTIVE ALLYSHIP

10

ON STAGE

Back in 2012 when I started my coaching business, I have to admit that I floundered a bit. I had always worked for organizations that provided me with regular paychecks. I had zero experience creating a new business from scratch. So I sought out advice from other coaches, from independent contractors, and from members of the women-in-tech community.

One recurring theme I heard was to get out and speak in public. To talk about my experience being a woman in the tech industry. To share my leadership stories. To become more visible. People told me it was a surefire way to start attracting coaching clients. Seems straightforward enough, right?

But here's the thing. While I had done some public speaking in the past—giving the occasional talk at a conference and leading my all-hands meetings as an executive—I didn't think I was good at it. Like most people, nerves got the best of me. I certainly didn't *enjoy* giving talks. And I really, really didn't want to do more of it.

Yet I embraced the advice because I realized it could be the key to growing my new business. So I set a goal for myself: Scary as it might be, I was going to speak in public once a month. Since then, I've met or exceeded that goal. In my busiest month, I spoke seven times. And get this: I've come to love public speaking.

In fact, I'm now a self-proclaimed public speaking geek. I've even coauthored a book on the topic, *Present! A Techie's Guide to Public Speaking,* with Poornima Vijayashanker, to help others learn this craft. I especially want to see more people from underrepresented groups giving talks at all-hands meetings at their companies, at local events, and on stage at larger industry conferences.

After all, public speaking is like a career multivitamin. Presenting at a team meeting, a company gathering, or an external event increases one's visibility. Which leads to sponsors taking notice. And that leads to career growth.

Of course, there's one additional benefit. By simply being more visible, speakers become role models for others who may be just a step or two behind them on their own career journeys. When newer, younger, or less experienced employees see people who look like them speaking, it empowers them to follow suit. Plus, when they're a member of an underrepresented group, they get to bust stereotypes about what a leader or expert looks like.

This is why I encourage allies to help people from underrepresented backgrounds do more public speaking. Here's what that might look like:

- During Q&A sessions at your all-hands meetings or external events, take the first question from someone from an underrepresented group. Doing so helps increase their visibility.

- Ask staff from marginalized groups to deliver project updates at staff meetings.
- Introduce them to conference organizers who are putting together panels or looking for speakers.
- Attend their dry runs as they practice their presentations, to show support and give them feedback so they can improve.
- If you're asked to do a keynote or speak on a panel, pass the opportunity along to someone on your team or in your network who's from an underrepresented group.
- Turn your keynote into a showcase, like Megan Smith (then chief technical officer of the United States and assistant to the president) did at the 2015 Grace Hopper Celebration. Instead of delivering the keynote herself, she asked six female colleagues from the U.S. Digital Service to join her on stage to share the work they were doing.[119]

Taking any of these actions will make you a better ally. But there's much more that allies can do to influence public speaking opportunities in a variety of settings. Let's explore them.

Homogeneous speaker lineups

In the not-so-distant past, some clever person coined the term "manel" to describe a panel consisting of only men. A panel that subconsciously reinforces that men are the experts; that women don't belong. And then there are "man-ferences"—conferences that feature all-male speaker lineups. And while I haven't yet come across a term for all-white panels, that's a problem too. Across industries, these exclusionary events have become an epidemic.

Even more problematic is when these speakers don't have direct lived experience of the topic. Such as panels about the challenges faced by women in tech featuring only men. Or discussions on transgender rights where all the panelists are cisgender people. Or interfaith panels with speakers who represent different Christian denominations but not other world religions.

As a panel organizer myself, I can see how easy it is to select a homogeneous group. Most organizers reach out to their network to find people who can speak on the topic. If they lack diversity in their network (which most people do, as we learned in Chapter 4), chances are they're going to lack diversity at the event. However, ensuring that speakers represent a variety of viewpoints and experiences can be a stretch goal for allies. It might be challenging, but it's important enough that all allies should be willing to move outside their comfort zones to make it happen.

Here's an example from my own career: Back when I was a vice president at Adobe, I was a member of our Engineering Council, a group of senior technical leaders across the company. One of our initiatives was sponsoring an annual internal technical conference. Typically we tapped two principal scientists to lead the yearly event, and they in turn would tap colleagues to run the various content tracks and review proposals from employees who wanted to speak.

One year, the two organizers (both white men) came to the Engineering Council with an update on their planning work. One of them announced, "We're proud of the diversity we've achieved with our committee. We have someone from each of Adobe's global offices." As he showed a slide with the employees' photos (all of whom were men), I quickly quipped, "I'm glad you've focused on diversity, but where are the women?" To their credit, they quickly admitted their mistake, and sheepishly explained that they didn't know who to ask. I offered to help identify some female track chairs. This was important to me, because I believed the female track chairs would, in turn, advocate for speaker diversity. And I was willing to create some public discomfort to ensure the lineup was more inclusive.

How can you help if you're an ally? Here's another story that might offer some inspiration.

In April of 2018, automation-in-testing advocate Richard Bradshaw showed his true colors as an ally. Upon discovering that the Code Europe conference he'd agreed to speak at had lined up only male speakers (a whopping eighty-seven of them), he promptly canceled. Richard then went on to create a "speaker rider" for himself that requires both a code of conduct and diverse speakers for any event at which he'll agree to present.

Now *that's* saying, "Not cool," with some stake in the game.

I encourage all allies reading this book to follow Richard's example. Before accepting a speaking engagement or panel slot, do the same type of vetting discussed back in Chapter 5 when we examined organizing and attending events. Events at which you speak should be held to the same standards, so do some preliminary digging. Does the event website show only white men, or is there a diverse group of people represented? Is there a posted code of conduct? If all signs point to an exclusionary event, ask the organizers for clarification. Questions like "Will there be any speakers or panelists of color?" or "Are you planning to have a code of conduct?" let the hosts know where your priorities lie. Your

inquiries may even prompt the organizers to make meaningful changes to their policies.

Refusing to sit on all-male or all-white panels is a simple
way for allies to express their desire to see this change. Allies
who want members of underrepresented groups to do more
public speaking must be willing to move aside and point the
spotlight at people with less privilege and access. Effective
allies lead by example.

Now, sometimes "leading by example" is code for
"avoiding conflict," but when it comes to being an ally, the
behaviors we model can have a noticeable ripple effect. After
Richard Bradshaw cancelled his appearance at Code Europe,
he tweeted about it and wrote a follow-up blog post, in which
he said:

> *How did I let this happen? Your name was on that conference
> page Richard, your company was on that page! I felt
> embarrassed. These thoughts came after cancelling my
> attendance, cancelling was a must, as a male speaker who cares
> about their craft, cares about inclusion, there was only one
> option, the right one. It was great to read a few replies later
> from some of the other male speakers cancelling their
> attendance.*[120]

Simply seeing Richard announce his cancellation
prompted other male panelists to follow suit. Just imagine the
domino effect if more male allies did the same.

If you're a speaker or event organizer, here are some ally
actions to take:

- **If you are asked to speak,** ask the organizer who else
  will be speaking on the panel or at the event. Review
  the list of speakers, if possible. If you see only people
  who look like you, push back like Richard Bradshaw
  did.

- **If you are an active public speaker,** refer colleagues from marginalized groups for the next request you get. Adam Singer, an analytics advocate at Google, had been giving about twenty-five talks each year, and in 2017 he decided to pass opportunities along to people he called "new voices." As a result, many of them became regulars on the speaking circuit.[121]
- **If you unexpectedly find yourself on a homogenous panel,** consider giving up your spot in the moment.
- **If you're organizing an event,** ask every male you're inviting to speak to recommend a woman, a person of color, or a member of another underrepresented group to also speak. And, as I recommended back in Chapter 1, take actions to diversify your network so you have a more varied group of people to tap for your next event.

Of course, panels and conferences aren't the only events where underrepresented voices should be amplified. Any gathering or meeting should be seen as a forum for diverse perspectives. And these principles can be applied to other kinds of inclusiveness: Everyone, of any identity, can ask if people of color; women, trans, and nonbinary people; and/or disabled speakers will be featured and push back if not. When we create more opportunities for members of marginalized groups to speak, even if it means keeping quiet ourselves, we are enabling equity on multiple levels.

Ask about the code of conduct

In Chapter 5 I discussed the importance of creating and enforcing codes of conduct, and the concept resurfaces when it comes to discussing the need to screen speaking engagements. Here's your gentle reminder to ask about an event's code of conduct before agreeing to deliver a presentation or sit on a panel.

After accepting a speaking gig

Of course, there are plenty of times when allies can and should speak. Whenever you serve as a speaker, you can be an effective ally by making sure that your presentations are inclusive and accessible to all.

For instance, Matt May, accessibility expert and head of inclusive design at Adobe, tweeted the following: [122]

Matt made an important point, and one that many speakers don't consider while running a Q&A session. It's also important to avoid using tiny fonts in presentation slides, so all audience members can see the content, and create visuals that are diverse and welcoming. (More on slide design in the next section.)

Ally actions don't stop with accessibility. When speakers with particular privileges or power are given the opportunity to address diverse audiences, it's their responsibility to be fully present and respectful.

Kat Gordon is the founder of the 3% Movement, whose mission is to change the ratio of creative directors from 3 percent to 50 percent. In June 2015, it hosted an event in London that included a "Manbassadors" panel where four men from the creative industry spoke about their commitment to diversity. Sounds pretty good, right? Well...

They showed up, bragged on stage, and immediately left to go to the hotel bar and drink together. They didn't listen to other speakers. They didn't take the opportunity to learn about the challenges facing women in their field. They didn't diversify their networks.

Kat was busy leading the event and didn't notice their absence. But if she had, she would have sent one of the good men who stuck around down to the bar to ask the other guys to embody true manbassadorship and come back to the event.

Even when allies can't or don't pass a speaking opportunity along to someone with less privilege or access, they can still comport themselves in ways that broadcast true allyship. And that includes showing respect to event organizers and attendees.

It also includes designing presentations that go beyond snapshots of smiling white dudes.

Creating inclusive slide decks

After the publication of my first book, my coauthor and I created a presentation to share its key messages and drive awareness (and hopefully sales). After we outlined our talk, I dove into designing a slide deck, using stock photography and other images to reinforce our speaking points. And I purposefully chose images of women, taking the opportunity to showcase diversity—or so I thought.

I believed I'd done a good job with our slides, until we delivered that talk at the Palo Alto Lean In Circle meeting in January 2016. My daughter Emma, who was in the audience, gave me feedback afterward. She pointed out that all of the stock photography was of white women, most of whom had blond ponytails. Jeepers. I hadn't even noticed. (As you might have guessed, I immediately changed the slide deck to reflect more diversity.)

By contrast, I remember being happily surprised as I watched Joel Spolsky, CEO of Stack Overflow, deliver a keynote at Pluralsight LIVE in 2017.[123] Want to know why? In his slides, when he showed photos of software developers, they were all women of color.

Think about the subtle—or not so subtle—messages you send wherever you use images. Not only in presentations and pitch decks, but also in your marketing collateral, in blog posts, and on your website. If you're showing only white, male, able-bodied people, what stereotypes are you reinforcing?

It may be understated, but the simple act of using stock photos of people from underrepresented groups makes a difference. And there are a handful of resources (many of which are free) to make it easy for you. I've listed several of my favorites in the "Additional Resources" section at the back of this book. Make them your go-to websites for finding stock photography whenever you need to show a photo of a professional person.

Speaking is power

Public speaking and panel participation are activities typically reserved for powerful, talented, accomplished people with important ideas. When exclusively white people, men, or white men perform those activities, the underlying message is that those people—and only those people—are worthy. Allies know and celebrate the fact that many nonwhite, nonmale people are powerful, talented, and accomplished. When called on to speak, allies use their privilege to ensure that more voices have a turn at the mic.

Actions for Better Allies:
Share Speaking Opportunities

Allies who are truly dedicated to amplifying marginalized voices must be willing to give up a few choice speaking gigs so others may share their knowledge.

- If you are a man and are asked to speak as part of an all-male lineup, push back and/or decline.

- When you do present, ensure that your slide images show people from a variety of backgrounds, gender identities, and abilities.

- If you're offered a speaking engagement but know someone from an underrepresented group who could knock it out of the park, connect them to the event organizer and pass on the spot yourself.

11

GIVING FEEDBACK

Wondering why we don't have more women in leadership roles across corporate America? Researchers at Stanford University's Clayman Institute can point to one of the reasons: the vague feedback that women tend to receive over their careers.

By analyzing performance reviews from three large tech companies and a professional services company, the researchers at Clayman uncovered some telling differences in the kind of feedback given to men versus women. They found that women were less likely than men to receive specific feedback tied to outcomes. This was true for both praise and constructive feedback. By contrast, men were offered a clearer picture of what they were doing well, how their performance was impacting the business, and what they needed to do to get promoted.[124]

The study also found other gendered differences in the performance reviews, specifically in the language used. When women were praised, they were twice as likely to receive feedback on team contributions versus individual accomplishments, which could hold them back during performance calibration and promotion discussions. Women were also described as "supportive," "collaborative," and "helpful" twice as often as men, and, interestingly, received 76 percent of the references of being "too aggressive." Men's reviews included words like "drive," "transform," "innovate," and "tackle" twice as often as women. Let's face it: The language used to describe men represents highly valued traits in many industries. The language used to describe women, on the other hand, is subjective and difficult to interpret.

I've seen some of this firsthand. A few years back, a tech company asked me to lead a career development workshop for a group of female employees. Beforehand, I was given access to their profiles and the kudos they'd received. One woman caught my eye because of two vastly different endorsements she received for the same project:

> "A big thanks to Sue for spearheading improvements to our product support portal. Very quick on the uptake and always responsive!"

> "Congratulations Sue on your 2-year anniversary at our company! You've done outstanding things in your first two years, including rebuilding the product support portal to scale with our $100M enterprise business."

As I read the first one, I felt it was superficial and rushed. The reviewer didn't identify how being "quick on the uptake" led to having an impact on customer satisfaction or bottom-line results. By contrast, the second reviewer clearly recognized Sue's impact: that she had rebuilt a key product, allowing the business to scale to $100 million.

The Stanford study isn't the only one to report disparities in how men and women receive professional feedback. Kieran Snyder, cofounder and CEO of Textio, applied linguistic analysis to performance reviews. She collected and analyzed 248 reviews from 180 people, including 105 men and 75 women from 28 different companies, in her study. Interestingly, 59 percent of the reviews received by men and 88 percent of those received by women contained critical feedback. And the suggestions given to women for improvement were more likely to focus on emotions, personality, and tone. Those given to men were more concrete, direct, and actionable.[125]

Shelley Correll and Caroline Simard of the Clayman Institute point out:

> *Clearly, these dynamics can disadvantage women at promotion time. Without specific, documented business accomplishments, it is difficult for a manager to make the case for advancement. Conversely, if a business objective was missed, a lack of frank feedback deprives women of the opportunity to hit the mark next time.*[126]

Of course, managers have to know about the larger business unit or corporate strategy in order to tie performance feedback to business outcomes. Unfortunately, not all managers do.

In 2017, I was coaching a group of women at a large tech company, leading a discussion on the importance of talking about the impact of our work. Many people, especially those who are early in their careers, tend to identify a long list of accomplishments when writing annual self-appraisals or updating their resumes. A better approach, as pointed out in the Clayman research, is to tie work to the business outcome by describing the impact of all these tasks. For example, instead of "fixed forty bugs," an engineer might write, "fixed all bugs blocking renewal sales of $5M." For the women I was coaching that day, this approach was novel—and, frankly, hard. Many didn't know why their manager prioritized certain tasks over others; many didn't know the higher-level goals of their division. So I encouraged them to ask their managers before our next meeting.

When we spoke about a month later, four of the fifteen women shared some striking news. Their managers were not able to answer questions about the business impact of their projects. And get this: Because those women didn't want to handicap their career growth, they immediately applied for an internal transfer. They wanted to work for managers who could be better allies by talking about the impact of their work and giving them feedback about how to have an even bigger impact.

How race and identity affect professional feedback

Gender bias is becoming more widely documented, but women are not the only group to receive mixed or misleading professional feedback. Within black communities, it's common for people to coach each other on the fact that they need to be "twice as good" as their white counterparts to achieve the same levels of success, and research shows that this is not far off. According to a study by Costas Cavounidis and Kevin Lang of Boston University, black workers receive extra scrutiny from their supervisors, which can lead to less favorable or constructive performance reviews, lower wages, and even job loss. With increased surveillance comes increased employee nervousness. Small mistakes are more likely to be caught, which over time leads to negative feedback and reduced pay. This research demonstrates how discrimination factors into company decisions, creating a feedback loop that results in ever-increasing racial gaps in the labor force.[127]

Gender identity and sexual orientation also affect workplace feedback. In a survey of LGBTQ Americans in 2017, 22 percent reported that they were not paid equally or promoted at the same rate as their straight and cisgender peers.[128] In 2015, 27 percent of respondents to a nationally representative survey of transgender people in the United States said they had experienced being not hired, fired, or not promoted due to their gender identity or expression.[129] And because many states offer no legal protection against workplace discrimination for LGBTQ individuals, people experiencing this bias frequently have no recourse.

The bottom line? When unconscious bias plays into performance appraisals and feedback, it can lead to inaccuracy and unfair treatment based on age, gender, race, ability, religion, appearance, sexual orientation, and other traits. Members of all underrepresented groups may struggle to obtain constructive, actionable feedback. And this means they will have a harder time improving their performance and advancing in their careers, keeping them from moving into visible roles and leadership positions. Without quality feedback, members of marginalized groups have a difficult time penetrating the upper echelons of workplace power.

Undoing bias about who "looks like a leader"

A 2018 study of performance reviews for more than four thousand leaders found that supervisors often assume women in leadership roles have communal qualities (e.g., being nurturing, relationship-focused, and collaborative), and that these are perceived to be less valuable than agentic characteristics (e.g., being instrumental, task-focused, and goal-oriented), which male leaders are assumed to possess. As a result, women don't "look like leaders" and get penalized for that. In an article for *Behavioral Scientist*, the study authors revealed the following insights:

> *Our findings suggest that people from underrepresented groups can be penalized for not looking like a leader, and are told implicitly that they are not leaders through the messaging of performance evaluations.*
>
> *As a result, women in leadership positions face an impossible situation. They will either receive feedback highlighting their lack of feminine, communal attributes ("She's not compassionate or organized enough"), criticizing them for taking too much power ("She's abrasive, overbearing"), or for lacking some key leadership qualification ("She's inept, temperamental"). No matter their leadership style, they are deemed unfit.*[130]

This particular study focused on a military academy and was performed by Naval Academy researchers, but their conclusions are supported by findings in the corporate world. Business consultancy Gartner has reported that qualified, diverse candidates are not getting due consideration for leadership roles, because of both unconscious and conscious bias in hiring and promotion decisions.[131] So many private companies pay lip service to the idea of a diverse workforce, yet hesitate to elevate people from underrepresented groups to management, leadership, or C-level positions. A lack of constructive feedback exacerbates the situation.

One piece of advice from the authors of the Naval Academy study? (Spoiler alert: You've heard this one already.) Be specific and clear about evaluation criteria. Doing so helps reduce bias and stereotyping based on personality traits.[132]

Avoiding gatekeeping

Anna Gifty, an undergraduate Mathematics/Economics major, tweeted that a professor tried to discourage her from pursuing a PhD in economics. The professor emphasized that "math is very difficult" and asked, "Are you sure you can handle the rigors of the discipline?"[133]

In sharp contrast, Dr. Patty Lopez responded with what she does in similar situations. "When someone asks me if they should try research, do something new, switch managers, change employers, I connect them to my network. #DontBeAGateKeeper."[134]

Gatekeeping feedback is common, and often slips out unconsciously. If you're in a position to give someone constructive comments, you may think you're doing so based solely on their performance or role, but your choice of words may betray unconscious bias. For instance, Harvard researchers examined teacher evaluations and found that men were more often described as "brilliant" and "genius" or praised for their innovative ideas, while women were more often acknowledged for their kind demeanor and execution.[135]

One quick way to check feedback for gatekeeping bias: Ask yourself, "Would I give the same feedback to someone of a different identity or background?" Kristen Pressner, who has worked as global head of human resources for Roche Diagnostics, gave a TEDx talk on bias and recommended the "flip it to test it" experiment, saying:

> *Maybe you are a superhuman person who manages to intercept those brain shortcuts at exactly the right moment to ensure you're behaving bias-free and consistently with your values, and beliefs, and all of your actions. It could very well be. But what have you got to lose to double-check yourself? If we all started to*

flip it to test it, we might just be surprised at how often we would choose to behave differently. Because what if you're missing an opportunity to see the world differently?[136]

Paying attention to pay

Did you know that women and employees of color receive less compensation than white men even when they receive equal scores on performance evaluations?[137] I wish I had known this back when I was an executive leading large software engineering teams. While I like to think that I awarded increases equitably, regardless of race and gender, this statistic makes me wonder.

I also wonder if there might have been a larger issue of pay inequity, based on employee's starting salaries or prior performance evaluations, that I could've addressed.

The problem is that many organizations still feel comfortable offering qualified female employees lower salaries. You've probably heard the stats about women earning less than their male counterparts, and that women of color earn even less. And you might have thought, "Okay, but that doesn't happen at my company." Well, are you sure? Here are just a few data points:

- Since 2000, U.S. income growth for black workers has been slower than for white workers in every wage bracket.[138]
- Women of color working in full-time, year round positions earn 63 percent of what white men earn, much less than the 79 percent that white women earn.[139]
- Female software engineers receive 83 percent of the salary that male software engineers receive.[140]

- Female financial managers earn 71 percent of what their male counterparts earn.[141]
- Female EMTs and paramedics earn 66 percent of what men are paid.[142]

When Salesforce CEO Mark Benioff heard concerns in 2015 that his company was paying women less than men, he was initially in denial. Yet a company audit uncovered a statistical difference in pay between genders. Mark admitted, "It was everywhere. It was through the whole company, every department, every division, every geography."[143] Over the next two years, Salesforce spent almost $6 million to close the gap.

Many other companies have since followed Salesforce's lead, including my former employer Adobe. Yet there is still work to do. Starting in April 2018, all companies that employ 250 or more people in the U.K. were legally required to reveal their gender pay gaps. And the reports weren't good. Many companies reported mean pay gaps of over 50 percent.[144]

Allies should also know that, in tech at least, as women gain experience their pay gap with men widens. Here's what this looks like: Within the first two years of working in tech, women ask for and receive 98 percent of what their male counterparts make. Then, with thirteen or fourteen years of experience, women ask for 94 cents for every dollar and *receive* just 92 cents for every dollar that men make.[145] Over time, the impact can be staggering. For example, imagine two equally qualified, thirty-five year old software engineers, one male and one female. Let's assume the man's annual salary is $150,000, and the woman earns 92 percent of that, or $138,000. That means the woman is earning $1000 less than the man every month. (Wow.) Now, assume they work for thirty more years, both receiving a three percent cost of living increase each year and no other raises. By the time they retire at age 65, the man will earn almost $30,000 more than the woman annually. Adding up the income difference each year over the thirty years, the man will have earned $600,000 more than the woman, not counting additional benefits that might be tied to base salary, such as bonuses or employee stock purchase programs.

While this widening gap issue may not hold true in all industries, women face pay-related obstacles no matter where they work. And their lifetime earning potential suffers. A multi-industry study shows that women ask for raises just as often as men, but are less likely to get them.[146]

If your company hasn't already instituted a pay equity review, you've got work to do. Do you have the power to make this happen for your team—or, better yet, for your larger function or business unit? If so, use your privilege to move your organization toward pay equity. And just like when giving feedback, be sure to use objective criteria to help curb biases when evaluating requests for increased salary or responsibility.

Why feedback matters and how to do it right

In 2016, McKinsey and LeanIn.Org performed a survey and found that women are less likely than men to receive difficult feedback—almost 20 percent less likely. Why? The study uncovered a number of reasons, including:

- It can be difficult to give constructive feedback because we don't want to upset someone. And this is especially true for male managers giving feedback to female employees.
- It can also be uncomfortable to give feedback to someone who is different from us—not just another gender, but a different race, sexual orientation, or

educational background. We might think, "If I point out how Mei, a graduate of a coding bootcamp, could have done a better job fixing that bug, she might think I'm biased against people who don't hold college degrees in computer science." To avoid this perception, we might soften the feedback.[147]

In her book *Radical Candor*, Kim Scott explores why it may be harder for men to be radically candid with women. She writes, "Most men are trained from birth to be 'gentler' with women than with men. Sometimes this can be very bad for the women who work for them."[148] In other words, men might hold back from criticizing female employees because they're afraid they might cry.

Kim reminds us that criticism is a gift, and that it needs to be given out in equal measures to all employees. Sounds good, but how do we actually make it so? If your company isn't already offering training on how to give feedback equitably, ask about it.

Whether your company has such training or not, here are some suggestions from the Clayman Institute for how supervisors can be more effective in evaluating employees equitably and giving them feedback:

- Identify criteria you'll use to evaluate employees at each level, and apply that criteria consistently.
- With each employee, discuss how their work has impacted the business.
- Tie all feedback, both positive and constructive, to business goals. For example, instead of just "Become a more strategic leader," you could say, "Become a more strategic leader by better understanding our competition and making recommendations to gain market share."

- Tell employees about the expertise you see them already exhibiting, and how they can develop more job-related skills.
- Write reviews of similar lengths so that you give roughly the same level of detailed feedback to all employees.[149]

Evaluating employees on inclusive behavior

As your company identifies objective criteria for evaluating employees, consider measuring how inclusive employees are. The more feedback people receive on inclusivity, the more it will become an ingrained behavior for them. Software engineer Chelsea Troy lays it out clearly in "A Rubric for Evaluating Team Members' Contributions to an Inclusive Culture":

- Does the employee effectively moderate meetings, encouraging all to participate, giving the floor back to anyone who is interrupted, and so on?
- Do they solicit opinions to understand diverse perspectives on an issue?
- Do they attribute others when they've built on someone's idea, learned from another person, or delivered something successfully with others' help?
- Do they assume coworkers are highly capable, and not condescend by offering unsolicited or unnecessarily basic advice?
- Do they capitalize on disagreements, effectively leveraging multiple perspectives to find the best solution?[150]

One last thing

Feedback is a two-way street. Allies can check in with their team and let them know they're working to become a better ally for underrepresented groups. They can ask, "What's one thing I could be doing differently to better support you or to create a more inclusive workplace?" And then they can take action.

> ## Actions for Better Allies:
> ### Give Effective and Equitable Feedback
>
> Feedback can be tricky to give, but it truly is a gift to receive. Without clear feedback, members of marginalized groups will have a much harder time succeeding and advancing. So, as an ally, remember:
>
> - When giving feedback, focus on the business impact of an employee's work. What should they keep doing because it's moving the business forward? How should they improve in order to have an even bigger impact?
>
> - Don't ease up just to avoid hurt feelings. Remember, vague feedback holds people back from growing in their careers.
>
> - Tell them about the expertise you see in them and how to develop more job-related skills.
>
> - Use objective criteria to evaluate employees in similar roles.
>
> - Write reviews of the roughly the same length for everyone on your staff.
>
> - Ask for feedback on how you can be a better ally.

12

OPENING CAREER DOORS

During the late 1980s, my partner Tim and I both worked at an applied research center at Brown University. Because of the economic recession at the time, the center's funding from corporate partners started to dry up, and we knew we were facing a downsizing. So we offered our resignations and decided to follow a dream we shared—to move to England, where Tim had spent his early childhood.

Soon after giving our notice to resign, my manager, Norm Meyrowitz, approached me with some exciting news. He had just met with two researchers who were visiting from a suburb of London, mentioned that I was moving there, and strongly recommended they hire me. (Knowing Norm, he probably told them they'd be stupid not to.) He could have been bitter about my resignation, but instead he opened a door for me, both literally and figuratively. He brought me into the conference room to meet them, and I joined their research group about two months later.

Fast forward five years and Tim and I were living in the San Francisco Bay Area. I was working as a localization manager for Macromedia when I became pregnant with our first child. There came the morning when I looked in the mirror at my expanding waistline and realized it was time to tell my coworkers. Later that day, I had a one-on-one meeting with our vice president, Joe Dunn. He started by saying, "Karen, I have an opportunity to tell you about. I want you to run the quality engineering team for the company, and it comes with a promotion to the director level."

I didn't miss a beat, and responded, "That sounds great—and by the way, I'm pregnant, I want to take four months of maternity leave, and when I come back, I want to work part-time." I remember his response to this day. It was an enthusiastic, "*Cool!*" His support was outstanding.

And then there was the time I knew someone acting as my sponsor had opened the equivalent of double French doors for my career. Years had passed, I was now a vice president of engineering at Macromedia, and the company was being acquired by Adobe. I attended a meeting with several members of Adobe's leadership team, and during a break one of them approached me and said, "Karen, I've really been looking forward to meeting you. Let's find time to talk soon about expanding your role and responsibilities once we complete the acquisition." Clearly, someone had been paying me some major compliments behind my back. It was sponsorship at its finest. I never discovered who my sponsor was, but I was so grateful they used their political clout to talk about me and open this major career door. I went on to work for that Adobe executive, with a much bigger role than I'd had before the acquisition.

These are just some examples of how allies have opened career doors over the course of my career. This type of support can take many shapes in addition to the ones I've described here. As I discussed in the previous chapter, giving the right kind of feedback can help someone grow their career. But it's also important to ask about career goals and share them with influencers, give stretch assignments and other learning opportunities, provide recommendations and referrals, and advocate effectively during performance calibration meetings and promotion discussions.

Career advancement support from allies can also take the form of seeing opportunities where others might see walls. Rachana Bhide, a talent leader and broadcaster for Bloomberg, collects stories from women about their male allies. In her Corner of the Court series, I read about Dr. Oksana Malysheva and Geoffrey Frost, a former CMO of Motorola. Oksana wrote, "Three weeks after my daughter was born, I received a phone call from Geoffrey. He right away launched into the project he wanted me to lead, and the promotion that came with it. I was excited but honest with him about my need to be with my daughter." Pushing past the walls she was constructing in her mind, Geoffrey focused on the flexibility and autonomy of the new role, and why it would be the perfect position for her as a new mother.[151]

Avoiding assumptions about career goals

I bet that Geoffrey was familiar with Oksana's career goals, and identified that opportunity for her as a result. However, I've heard too many stories describing situations where this hasn't been the case. For example, my coaching client who was working on a fast-growing engineering team when the team's leader identified the need for a project manager to keep all their work on track. He asked my client, the only woman on the team, to take on this role. It might have been an awesome opportunity, except that it wasn't at all aligned with her career goal to become a software quality manager.

I heard from Jenny, a vice president of engineering, who, when her role was eliminated, received advice from her manager that she take an individual contributor role in the marketing department. It was a big step down in terms of responsibility and pay, and it felt like a slap in the face to her. Jenny's manager assumed she would take any job to stay on the payroll. Instead of helping her find a role, even externally, that would align with her goals and leverage her leadership experience, he nudged her toward voluntary demotion.

As my friend Julie Kratz, founder of gender equality firm Pivot Point Consulting, shared with me: "For allies, it's all about listening to what she wants and not advising her. I think men jump the gun often and want to 'save the day,' rather than create a win-win for both." Julie then told me she had just spoken to a male ally that morning. He leads a large marketing team and recently reached out to high-potential women in the company about a new role on his team. All of them turned him down because they didn't want the travel that would come with the job. Julie encouraged him to have a deeper conversation: Ask what they wanted to do in three years, discuss options for how he could be flexible regarding travel, and identify how this opportunity would be an ideal assignment to allow them to build skills needed to help them reach their career goals.

Because of ingrained workplace dynamics, it may be necessary for allies to do more than offer opportunities or ask general questions. Sometimes, allies need to help promising candidates from underrepresented groups articulate their goals by reflecting on their worries. Sometimes allies need to be sounding boards before they can become door-openers.

The best stretch assignments are glamour work

Let's face it: Not all assignments are created equal. As Joan C. Williams and Marina Multhaup, researchers at the Center of WorkLife Law at the University of California, point out, "Some can set you up for promotion and skyrocket you to the top of your company—we call them glamour work. Other assignments are necessary but unsung. We call them office housework." And their research shows that women and people of color often wind up with worse assignments than their white male counterparts. Men get the glamour work while women and people of color get stuck with office housework. (Which, as we learned in Chapter 8, hinders their ability to be promoted.)[152]

What does glamour work look like in practice? More often than not, it's high profile. It might be developing an innovative product that is being sponsored by a senior vice president. Or joining a task force to identify new revenue streams, giving a keynote on behalf of one's company, or doing groundbreaking research.

But it can also include lower-profile stretch assignments that provide the opportunity to learn new skills and achieve better positioning for a promotion. Such assignments can also help increase confidence, enhance social networks, and build credibility across an organization. As a result, stretch assignments can help retain employees from underrepresented groups. These challenging or prominent assignments may even keep them from dropping out of the field completely.[153]

Given all these benefits, allies should leverage glamour work to open career doors for marginalized colleagues. And if allies truly want to both cultivate and *retain* a diverse workforce, assigning these choice projects to people from underrepresented groups will further that goal. So why, as those researchers from the Center of WorkLife Law found, do men get a higher portion of glamour assignments?

Perhaps it comes down to our networks. If managers don't know marginalized colleagues and their career goals, how would they know to tap them for these career-building opportunities? (If this is the case for you, go back to Chapter 4 for actions to diversify your network.)

Or is it because it's convenient to hand off office house-work to the people who first come to mind (often women), thereby giving men more time to build skills that will make them better candidates for glamour work? (Review Chapter 8 to avoid this tendency.)

Regardless of the reason, allies can turn this tide.

The next time you need someone to stand in for you on an initiative or take on a high-profile assignment, reflect on your selection criteria. Do you tend to give glamour work to certain people or certain types of people? What would it take to expand that pool? If you know only a few people who have the skills you value for these plum assignments, you might need to expand your network. Or figure out how more people, especially people outside your normal go-to list, can learn more of those skills. Glamour work is desirable work, work that opens doors and ignites careers. It's essential for allies to find ways to spread that joy around.

The role mentors play

Here's a surefire way to make sure more people in your professional network have the skills to tackle glamour work: mentor them. Or ask someone who has the right skills to mentor them. And to be a better ally, focus on mentoring people from underrepresented groups.

Not only will mentees learn skills, they may also feel more engagement with your company, which will help them become more successful overall. As I learned from Brad Johnson and David Smith in their book, *Athena Rising*, students at the Naval Academy rely on their upper-class mentors to pass along "the gouge"—salient tips for surviving, thriving, and avoiding big trouble. Mentors aren't just there to build confidence in their mentees; they can help prepare them for new challenges by sharing their own experiences and wisdom.

Which begs the question: Are members of under-represented groups at your company receiving the equivalent of "the gouge"? Do they have access to mentors willing to give them the inside scoop?

If not, they may feel hamstrung. Bloomberg reported that among eight of the largest U.S. tech companies, the portion of black workers in technical jobs was just 3.1 percent in 2017. And that number had barely shifted since 2014, when it was 2.5 percent.[154] While many factors contribute to these numbers, one of them could be that black workers feel left out of "the know." They may never have been mentored on how to thrive, or counseled on staying connected to key networking activities. They may not be in the loop on important discussions or have influential friends who can recommend their work.

One thing white allies can do to change this cultural tendency is mentor people of color at their companies. Is this you, but you're not sure where to start? If you have an employee group for people of color, reach out to its leadership and ask for advice about your next steps. Do your part to ensure that all promising employees are in the know, regardless of background.

Here's another idea, especially if patents are important to your company's strategy.

In July 2018, Fast Company published a story that started with: "In today's installment of unsurprising-yet-still-depressing news: Women of color, particularly black and His-panic women, are less likely to obtain U.S. patent rights than white women and men."[155]

Allies can actively work to change this ratio by encouraging women of color to file patents for the work they're doing, and by mentoring them along the way. Or consider what a staff engineer at Intel did to scale her efforts beyond just one mentee. She started a quarterly workshop on the company's patent-filing process to demystify it for everyone, but especially women.

Getting more women involved with patent work is not only good for their careers, it's also good for business. Research by the National Center for Women in Information Technology shows that mixed-gender teams produced the most frequently cited software patents—with citation rates 26% to 42% higher than the norm for similar patents.[156] What does this mean? Patent filings cite other patents to reference prior art that they've built on or to differentiate themselves. A patent that is cited frequently may be core to its field, meaning that it represents significant innovation. Simply stated, you're more likely to create a significant patent if you have a gender-diverse team.

Giving wholehearted recommendations

Recommendations come in many forms. Formal letters, social media endorsements, verbal reference checks, and back channel casual conversations can all impact the career trajectories of the people they describe. This means that when you're giving any kind of recommendation, you should show complete confidence. No hedging ("she might be good"), faint praises ("she'll do okay"), or other phrases that undermine ("she needs only minimal guidance").

Wondering why I'm calling this out? Turns out that in a 2018 study of recommendations for academic positions, researchers found that letters about women included more doubt-raising phrases than those about men, and that even one such phrase can make a difference in a job search.[157] This means that a lukewarm recommendation may be more harmful than no recommendation at all.

After sharing this research on Twitter, I heard from a professor who wrote:[158]

> **Tom Hartley** @tom_hartley · Oct 8   ⌄
> Reading some of my draft references, I sometimes think that even a solitary 'but' (connecting two otherwise unambiguously positive sentences) is enough to introduce doubt...

The next time you give someone a recommendation, make it a wholehearted one. Focus on the person's traits and accomplishments that are overwhelmingly positive and praise them to the skies. Otherwise, you risk shutting a door you intended to open.

Promoting on potential

Effective allies recognize and nurture raw talent in *all* of their employees. Findings from both McKinsey and the Catalyst Group found that "men get promoted based on potential and women get promoted based on performance."[159] This means that women are stuck on a treadmill, constantly proving and reproving that they're worthy of responsibility and capable of leadership. In fact, when women did all the things they were told would help them get ahead—using the same tactics as men—they still advanced less than their male counterparts and had slower pay growth.[160]

This tendency illustrates what's known as "prove it again" bias. Groups that have been stereotyped as less competent or hardworking often have to provide a larger, more compelling body of evidence in order to be judged as equally competent. Groups that have to "prove it again" include women, African Americans, Latinx people, individuals with disabilities, and Asian Americans. While a white man may only need to show promise in order to secure a promotion, a Latina employee may need to make a long and convincing case for herself to even be considered for advancement. Members of "prove it again" groups are often labeled as "not ready" for promotion, which can be code for unconscious bias. When promoting managers find themselves describing certain candidates as "not ready," they should consider whether they're expecting those folks to provide more evidence of competence.[161]

More evidence that men are immune from "prove it again" bias: They're more likely to get what they want without even having to ask. According to the 2017 "Women in the Workplace" study:

> *Women of all races and ethnicities negotiate for raises and promotions at rates comparable to their male counterparts. However, men are more likely to say they have not asked for a raise because they are already well compensated or a promotion because they are already in the right role.*[162]

While women are repeatedly asked to illustrate competence through performance, men get access to advancement opportunities without having to ask for them. While women must prove their worth, men are promoted simply for showing potential.

So how do allies recognize potential in their employees, regardless of gender, background, or identity? How can allies combat "prove it again" bias and learn to see promise in their colleagues and direct reports?

Psychologists Tomas Chamorro-Premuzic and Seymour Adler, along with leadership author Robert B. Kaiser, found that traits like enthusiasm and success-centric mind-sets are considered desirable by corporate leaders, but don't actually indicate that an employee has high potential. Their study showed that the following three markers of high potential are the ones to look for:

1. **Ability:** Is the candidate capable of doing the job in question? Is the candidate clearly able to learn and master the requisite knowledge and skills needed to perform this job?
2. **Social skills:** Does the candidate excel at teamwork and collaboration? Can the candidate manage both themself and others?
3. **Drive:** Is the candidate willing to work hard, achieve, and do whatever it takes to get the job done?[163]

Clearly, people of all genders and backgrounds can possess all three of these traits. "Ability" only becomes dicey if a promoting manager insists that a certain candidate prove again and again that they have what it takes. If you are an ally who is hoping to evaluate an employee from an under-represented group for a promotion, consider these three criteria instead of relying entirely on your gut. (Guts can be biased!) And if you are in a position to sit on a calibration or promotions board, and you don't know all of the candidates, take the time to get to know them. Once you do, find ways to scope and recognize their potential instead of insisting they prove their worthiness through performance.

How a simple nudge can open a door

In his book *Work Rules*, Laszlo Bock describes a problem Google was facing: Its female employees were less likely to nominate themselves for promotions, despite a policy that allowed all employees to do so.[164] The company found that a small nudge made a huge difference. All it took was senior vice president Alan Eustace sending an email to employees citing research about classroom dynamics, where boys tend to raise their hand to answer any question, where girls tend to wait to be certain. With that nudge, not only did application rates from women soar, the volume of their promotions even surpassed those of their male counterparts.[165]

Allies don't need to be in a position to directly promote marginalized employees. Think about providing support from the sidelines. Just encouraging them, nudging them to push forward in their careers, can make a huge difference.

Layers of bias can form doorstops

In 2018, the Kapor Center ran a pilot study on the challenges facing female tech entrepreneurs, including the myriad biases women face when raising capital. The researchers also studied how race factors in, with women of color reporting substantially worse experiences than white women. One statistic caught my eye: "Women of color were more than 3 times as likely to report bullying than white women (75% versus 22%), and nearly 10 times as likely to report experiencing non-consensual touching (38% vs 4%)."[166] Let that sink in. It's a not-so-subtle reminder that intersectionality must be taken into account when we create promotion strategies and diversification efforts.

As you think about how to open career doors, realize that not all women face the same challenges, and that women of color may need different support and allyship because of the additional and compounded bias and harassment they confront.

One last thing

In 2017, I attended the Calibrate Conference in San Francisco. Jill Wetzler, then director of engineering at Lyft, gave an inspiring talk titled "The Inclusive Leader: Developing Diverse Teams."[167] One of the many excellent tips she gave was to encourage listeners to sponsor protégés who are not like them. Speak their names when they aren't around. Endorse them publicly. Share their interests with influencers. Champion them.

Think about who you sponsor. If they tend to be "like you" or remind you of your younger self, consider developing relationships with a more diverse group of protégés—and start opening some doors for them.

Actions for Better Allies:
Don't Be a Gatekeeper, Be a Door Opener

Helping people from underrepresented groups achieve their goals and advance their careers is one of the most powerful things allies can do. Here's how:

- Ask the people you manage or mentor about their career goals and, with permission, share them with influencers.

- Be equitable when handing out stretch assignments and other learning opportunities.

- Give wholehearted recommendations and referrals.

- Advocate effectively during performance calibration meetings and promotion discussions.

- Nudge colleagues from marginalized groups to pursue career growth opportunities.

- Sponsor people who are not like you. Speak their name when they aren't around. Endorse them publicly.

13

A CALL TO ACTION

In August 2017, we recorded another milestone on the unofficial "lousy tech diversity timeline"— a timeline that is all too full of events about sexism, bias, misogyny, creepy behavior, and harassment. It's timeline that shouldn't exist, but does.

That's when Google engineer James Damore wrote an internal memo criticizing his company's diversity and inclusion efforts. In the ten-page screed, he argued that differences in pay between men and women in the technology sector are not rooted in bias against women but instead are attributable to biological differences between the genders.[168] In doing so, he made plenty of people angry, but also validated the secretly held beliefs of others: that diversity efforts are pointless, that women simply aren't good scientists, and that the best will rise to the top naturally. And that the best are men—usually white men.

When the story of his memo broke over the weekend, social media channels lit up. Myriad posts. Twitter fistfights.

Blogged responses. Attention from the press. I couldn't pull myself away.

That said, I also found it draining. And I started to realize the challenge that women across the tech industry would face as they returned to work on Monday morning. Wondering if any of their teammates agreed with that memo, in part or in full. Wondering if they would need to debate their right to their chosen profession.

Unfortunately, more milestones get added to this unofficial "lousy tech diversity timeline" periodically. Not long after the Google manifesto, #MeToo became a full-fledged movement with repercussions in multiple fields, including tech. Despite the fact that women held a mere 18 percent of all physics doctoral degrees in 2017, physicist Alessandro Strumia of the University of Pisa delivered a presentation explaining how the field of physics discriminates against men.[169] In mid-2018, Stuart Reges, a University of Washington computer science lecturer, argued that women would never make up more than 20 percent of tech employees, likely because boys are better at math and science, and girls are better at reading.[170] The list goes on.

And, of course, biases against underrepresented groups remain prevalent in fields besides tech. Consider how Serena Williams was treated at the 2018 U.S. Open finals, where she was penalized for expressing her frustration on the court. Multiple male tennis players came forward to say they'd said and done much worse during their matches and never been criticized. Management scholar and author Adam Grant summed it up perfectly by saying, "When a man argues with an umpire, it's passion. When a woman does it, it's a melt-down. When a black woman does it, it's a penalty."[171]

Incidents of victim blaming and character assassination are widespread as well. It seems that little has changed since

1991, when Anita Hill accused Clarence Thomas of harassment during his U.S. Supreme Court hearings. We saw history repeat itself with Dr. Christine Blasey Ford's brave testimony against Brett Kavanaugh in 2018. Setting aside political leanings, there's an underlying cautionary tale for better allies everywhere: to not blame our colleagues or assassinate their character when they raise issues or file formal complaints.

Chances are, more examples have been added to this timeline since I published this book. Sometimes, the struggle for equity in the workplace can feel like taking two steps forward only to be forced three steps back. But there are things allies can and should do to surge ahead.

Speak up and speak out

With each incident of inequity, allies have an opportunity to support colleagues who are more impacted than themselves. Effective allies not only say that they believe in these colleagues, but they also demonstrate it and show them that they think differently than the author of a leaked memo, the administrator in charge of a harmful policy, or the biased thought leader.

Allies have a duty to speak up, speak out, and take action. Here are some ideas on how to do so:

- Tell coworkers that you believe in workplace diversity and you're glad to be working with or for them.
- Express gratitude to coworkers, calling out specific behaviors you appreciate. For example, "I like the way you describe architectural risk during code reviews."
- Talk about specific things you've learned from coworkers. For example, "What I learned from Maria about AI open source libraries is …"

- Tell coworkers about the expertise you see in them and how awesome they are.
- Challenge biased behavior when you see it. Don't be a bystander, be an upstander. Take action.
- Advocate for systemic changes to address non-inclusive behavior. Don't act as a knight to "save" one marginalized person. Instead, drive change that will help all marginalized individuals and create a more inclusive culture.

Commit to sponsoring four people

Toward the end of 2017, author and management expert Tom Peters tweeted, "Bosses: Who are the four folks whose development path you will have dramatically affected by 12/31/18?"[172] Unable to resist such a perfect setup, I replied, "Plot twist: Who are the four women or underrepresented humans whose development path you will have dramatically affected by 12/31/18? #MaleAllies."

My challenge to allies is to identify four women or members of other underrepresented groups to sponsor in the current or coming year. And by sponsor, I mean do things like:

- Speak their name when they're not around
- Share their career goals with influencers
- Recommend them for stretch assignments
- Talk about what you've learned from them
- Invite them to high-profile meetings
- Give them your speaking slot at an event
- Endorse them publicly

Even if mentoring feels like an overwhelming time commitment at this point, you can start by sponsoring. Being visible and vocal in your support of those with less privilege and access is leading by example.

Define or refresh your values

Although I want this book to focus on actions that stretch allies beyond thinking, there is definitely a place in this call-to-action chapter for self-reflection. Change starts with each of us as individuals. So we should ask ourselves: How do we want to operate? Treat people? Would we turn down business or investments because of creepy behavior? Would we dismiss our top sales executive after disciplining him for harassment? What are the deals we won't do because they conflict with our values? When will we walk away from cash?

How allies treat colleagues from marginalized groups in the workplace must stretch beyond meeting protocols and everyday language, and toward activities that impact the bottom line. Allyship becomes meaningless if it's abandoned in the face of lucrative business deals or strategic partnerships. Committed allies remember their values and live them out.

Continue the journey

Being an ally is a journey. I hope you'll join me. For ongoing ideas, subscribe to my weekly newsletter "5 Ally Actions" on betterallies.com, and follow @betterallies on Twitter, Medium, Instagram, and/or Pinterest.

Together, we can—and will—make a difference.

BONUS CHAPTER

INTERVIEWING WHILE WHITE AND MALE

Steve Tannock, a technology architect, recently asked me this question: "Perfectly selfishly: I'm a middle-aged white guy who generally only wants to work with/for orgs doing good diversity work. But hiring me is almost the opposite of that. Suggestions for reconciling/approaching this?"

Many people with privilege feel the same way as Steve. If this is you, here are five suggestions, not only to help you land that next job but *also* to further diversity and inclusion along the way.

Emphasize what you've done to build and support diverse teams

Kristen Pressner, a global HR executive who speaks about the power of #FlipItToTestIt, had this advice for Steve and others in positions of privilege because of their race, gender, or other factors: "Flip it from assuming that you don't have a 'diversity value' to what value you can add. Emphasize what you've done in the past to build diverse teams and how you've supported them to be successful."[173]

I love this advice. Not only does it allow a candidate to shine a positive light on their past experience, it could also give the interviewers an idea or two about how they could be better allies. Win-win!

Talk about your dedication to mentoring women

David Smith, coauthor of *Athena Rising*, provided this advice for Steve: "Gender inclusion is not a women's issue to solve—it is the organization's issue. Share how you've mentored and sponsored women and how you'll continue to do so in your next role."[174]

This is especially important in the context and aftermath of the #MeToo movement. Men shouldn't retreat from mentoring women. Ditto for mentoring members of other underrepresented groups. We need everyone working in support of diversity and inclusion.

Know your diversity adversity story

Even if you check lots of privilege checkboxes, you've probably faced some adversity. Jennifer Brown, author of *Inclusion*, recommends: "Identify your diversity story—about a time you faced the sting of exclusion. Be vulnerable. Share it to model the value you place on inclusive workplace practices."[175]

One example of this is a senior leader who had been covering up the fact that he didn't hold a college degree. Once he started sharing this story, he became more approachable and was a role model for alternative education paths for his employees.

Ask what the company is doing to create an inclusive workplace

Interviewing is a two-way street. Be sure to ask the interview team about why diversity and inclusion are important to them, and what the company is doing in this area. Cath Jones, a people operations professional, shared this advice for Steve:

> I *always find it valuable to ask what policies and processes they have in place. If they are heading down the right track they will be thinking about things like inclusion, the gender pay gap, physical accessibility of the office etc. If not you can normally gauge by [their] response how open they are to improvement. We need people at the top to guide the way and advocate for others. A good organisation won't have an issue that you aren't a minority but they will want to know that you share their values.*[176]

If you join that company, you'll be in a position to check that it's actually living its values—that it's committed to offering an inclusive workplace. And you can hold leaders accountable if they're straying from that goal.

Be vulnerable and share a mistake you made on your journey to be a better ally (and what you learned from it)

We've all been there. Wanting to show our support for diversity, but saying the wrong thing. Or writing a quick message and using gendered language by mistake. Or laughing at an off-color joke. You know what I'm talking about. Perhaps you've been a bystander who ignored some sexist or otherwise offensive behavior, and in hindsight, you know you should have called it out.

Turns out there's a growing number of veterans using #IWasWrong to share how they were complicit in the culture of misogyny in the U.S. Armed Forces.

As you prep for your next interview, think about your #IWasWrong story. A time when you were complicit, when you didn't take action to support someone from a marginalized group, when you didn't push back against non-inclusive behaviors. And what you learned from that experience about how to be a better ally. It's a great way to answer the classic interview question, "Tell me about a time you made a mistake, and how you handled it."

One last thing

For those of you on the other side of the interview table, be sure to ask candidates about how they've contributed to creating a more inclusive workplace. And if you're interviewing them for a management role, ask about prior experience building and leading diverse teams, as discussed in Chapter 6.

EPILOGUE

THE BINGO CARD THAT STARTED IT ALL

I did not attend the Grace Hopper Celebration in 2014. Instead, I watched the keynotes that were streamed online, and I followed along on social media.

In the days leading up to the event, a buzz started building on Twitter about the male allies panel that was a scheduled feature of the conference. Complaints were surfacing about men taking the stage away from women at a women's conference, and questions were raised. If these panelists were such great allies for women, why didn't their companies have better diversity?

And then I saw a tweet that caught my eye.

A group calling themselves "The Union of Concerned Feminists" created a bingo card with phrases they expected to hear from the panelists, phrases that would show that these men still had a long journey ahead of them before they became true male allies.[177] They handed out the bingo card to the audience. And about halfway through the panel, a young woman shouted out, "Bingo."

A L L Y   B I N G O

We are glad that men are talking about supporting women in tech. But GHC is already full of women! Being an ally means confronting oppressive behavior *when you're around people in the majority group*, not explaining to a bunch of women how *totally* not sexist you are, and how your company has changed (we're looking at you, GoDaddy, and your multi-billion-dollar IPO aspirations). With that, we present to you many of the things you are about to hear in this panel, because we've heard it all before. BINGO TIME!

Name drops Sheryl Sandberg	"That would never happen in my company"	Calls a woman articulate	Refers to a feminist as aggressive / angry / offputting	Blames "awkward geeks" for abusive behavior in tech
Wearables. Women like wearing things, right?	"Ask any woman I know, she'll tell you I'm a feminist"	Teaches girls to code but won't mentor women	Quotes woman he has power over in the workplace	Ignorant of employment equity legislation
Corporate redemption narrative	Wants a cookie for basic decency	~~PIPELINE~~	"I asked a woman and she agreed with me"	Asserts other man's heart is in the right place
"I am related to a woman" / Saw the light after birth of daughter	"If GoDaddy can change, anyone can"	Says feminist activism scares women away from tech	My mother taught me to respect women	"I've believed in women's rights my whole life"
"We're all in this together"	"Men's voices need to be heard too"	Quotes MLK, gets meaning reversed	"I consider myself an equalist / humanist"	Lean In

During the Q&A session, here are some suggestions for questions to ask of these dudes:
- Have you conducted a pay equity audit, and if so, what were the results?
- How do your rates of promotion compare between women and men?
- Which efforts to reduce sexism at your company target men's behavior?
- What programs specific to retaining women do you have in place at your company?

This intervention brought to you by the **Union of Concerned Feminists**. Find us on Twitter at **@ConcernedFems**. Read more about actual feminism in technology, not the milquetoast corporate "feminism" you saw today, from some of our friends:

modelviewculture.com   geekfeminism.org   geekfeminism.wikia.com   adainitiative.org

Reprinted with permission of Leigh Honeywell

The bingo card was a hit. Perhaps because it highlighted that diversity initiatives are so often trite sound bites backed by little action. After all, three of the four companies represented on the panel had an employee pool in which fewer than twenty percent of the technical staff were women, so clearly they had a long way to go.

That said, I wondered if these men (and other men working across tech) would ever figure out how to be better allies.

So I decided to make an aspirational version. A bingo card with phrases I *wanted* to hear from men. Phrases that show they are taking a stand to improve diversity and not just paying lip service to it. Phrases that represented actions they could take to make a difference.

To make the bingo card, I partnered with another technologist, Cate Huston, who was at the panel and became heavily involved in pushing back against it, which led to a well-received "reverse panel" the next day for the men to listen to women's concerns. Together, Cate and I wrote and rewrote a series of aspirational phrases, editing and culling our list, and used an online bingo card generator to create the card.

I speak at conferences only if they have a code of conduct.	We did a salary review by gender and corrected inequities.	We track retention numbers of women in our engineering roles.	I publically recognize & reward women who are involved with helping other women.	We have published goals for improving our diversity numbers.
Our job descriptions include "experience working on a diverse team, with a diverse range of people."	I proactively work to amplify more women's voices.	I have a zero-tolerance policy of derogatory language in design documents and in code.	I refuse invitations to all-male panels.	Gender diversity is more than a just pipeline problem.
I have spoken up when women are discriminated against or excluded from activities.	I have banned the phrase "Hiring Bar."	**I am a feminist**	Our job descriptions list only required skills, not nice-to-haves.	We proactively address biased feedback in interviews and promotion cycles.
Our job descriptions list open source experience only when it is a true requirement.	We track time in role and promotion rates for underrepresented minorities.	I meet with women who file HR complaints so that I can understand the issues and support them.	I have encouraged other men to speak up when minorities are discriminated against or belittled in front of them.	I have been a sponsor to a woman.
I have been a peer mentor to a woman.	I have recommended a qualified women for opportunities I could not pursue myself.	I have invested in a female founder.	I have fired a person with privilege or power for being sexist.	I have read extensively including peer reviewed literature on unconscious bias.

Once it was done, we wanted to share it with the world. Cate secured a web domain to host it, and I started tweeting the phrases from a new Twitter account, @betterallies. Then we wrote about it for the *Daily Beast* in an article titled, "Tech's Male 'Feminists' Aren't Helping."[178]

Soon after we published that article, Kathryn Rotondo reached out, offering to edit and redesign the bingo card. I'm forever grateful for the work she did to turn our ugly duckling into this stunning design:

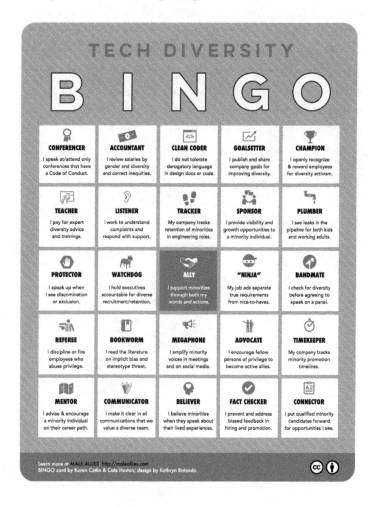

This project was my catalyst, the starting point on my journey for this book. And I'm deeply grateful to Cate Huston for partnering with me to create the bingo card, Kathryn Rotondo for her design and editing work, and Leigh Honeywell, the person behind the original bingo card at the 2014 Grace Hopper Celebration, for instigating it all.[179]

You can download the bingo card from betterallies.com. Consider printing it and posting it in a visible area of your workplace to generate awareness. Or hand it out at an event, like O'Reilly Media's Suzanne Axtell frequently does at technical conferences.

Interested in creating a bingo card for allies in your industry? Our design is offered under the Creative Commons Attribution 4.0 International license, which means you can distribute, remix, tweak, and build upon it as long as you credit us for the original creation, like The 3% Movement did in creating a "Manbassador Bingo Card" for the 2015 3% Conference in London.[180] Be sure to tell me if you make one by sending an email to info@betterallies.com or tagging @betterallies on Twitter. I'd love to see your creation.

Our journey continues.

RECAP: ACTIONS FOR BETTER ALLIES

Here's a compilation of the actions included at the end of each chapter.

Understand Your Privilege and Use It for Good

An important part of allyship is being open to learning, improving, and taking action.

- Review the list of fifty potential privileges in the workplace that was included in Chapter 1. How many apply to you?

- Identify at least one way you can be a better ally, using the archetypes in Chapter 1.

- Understand that being an ally is a journey. We all make mistakes. Don't let that hold you back from taking action.

Be an Ambassador for Change

Helping individuals is laudable, but the responsibility of allies is to take actions that will have lasting, beneficial effects on systems (as often as possible).

- When lending a hand to a single person, step back to look for systemic changes that will benefit many employees.

- Suggest new processes that will change ingrained behaviors and create a more inclusive culture.

- Pay attention to your motivations: Focus on what will authentically support marginalized people long-term, rather than what will make you feel or look good.

Listen, Believe, Learn

Being an effective ally includes the less forceful but equally important activities of listening to alternate perspectives, accepting the information that people from under-represented groups share, and learning from their stories and one's own mistakes.

- Be vulnerable and honest when you open discussions with colleagues who have less power and privilege than you.

- Resist the urge to get defensive.

- Review the list of red-flag phrases that was included in Chapter 3, and speak out when you hear them.

- Take action when you see or hear about bigotry, harassment, or discrimination. Be an upstander, not a bystander.

- Accept that yes, prejudice does exist in your own workplace.

Diversify Your Network

Most of us have largely homogeneous networks. Here are some tips for ensuring that your network is diverse and more effective:

- Do a network inventory. List out the people you feel to be your top ten contacts. Are any of them marginalized in ways that you are not? If not, start in your own backyard: Who within your own company could be a great addition to your current network?

- Attend an event where diversity will be the topic of discussion. Listen and learn.

- The next time you attend an event of *any* kind, introduce yourself to someone who doesn't look like you.

- If you are interested in attending an event that caters specifically to a group of which you are not a member, ask the organizers before showing up.

- Seek out media, including podcasts and blogs, by people who are different from you.

Make Events Welcoming

Too many professional events can be inhospitable for members of underrepresented groups. Here are some ways to help turn the tide:

- Make events inclusive. Feature diverse voices, offer interesting non-alcoholic drinks, create and enforce a code of conduct, practice full accessibility, provide financial assistance, and push back on risqué images and offensive swag.

- Before attending or agreeing to speak at an event, make sure there will be a code of conduct as well as other support for attendees from underrepresented groups.

- If you see a lineup of speakers that's homogeneous, contact the organizers and demand better.

- Look out for microaggressions (or worse) during an event, and take action when you spot them.

Strive to Hire Equitably

Allies can band together to banish the "leaky pipeline" excuses and focus on employing strategies that are proven to attract diverse applicants. Here are some ways you can make this possible in your own company:

- Look at your company's careers web page and job descriptions. Remove biased language, weed out any requirements that aren't needed, and find ways to appeal to people from different backgrounds.

- During your next recruiting push, challenge current employees to refer members of underrepresented groups from their networks for open positions.

- Implement structured interviews for open positions.

Amplify and Advocate in Meetings

At many companies, much of the workday is spent in meetings. This means that ensuring the voices of members of underrepresented groups are heard and valued is essential to creating an inclusive work culture.

- Challenge yourself to notice and take action when interruptions happen in meetings.

- Cultivate a culture of credit: Encourage everyone around you to acknowledge the originator of ideas as often as possible.

- Be vigilant and push back on off-topic questions and showboating.

- Take note of how attendees arrange themselves in meeting rooms. Do what you can to mix up seating arrangements so your marginalized coworkers are in power positions.

- Ask a back channel buddy to keep you accountable.

Share the Load

Office housework isn't just aggravating. Calling exclusively on women, people of color, and members of other marginalized groups to perform it means preventing them from tackling more meaningful work. With that in mind:

- Share the work among the team. For example, if you notice one person is always tasked with mentoring the summer interns, say something like, "Ann's great at mentoring. But it's the perfect stretch assignment for Nick, who has never done it before."

- Set up a rotation for tasks like taking minutes or scheduling the next meeting.

- If you're in a position of privilege or authority, model better behavior yourself by clearing the lunch leftovers or used coffee mugs, rather than assuming someone else will take care of it.

- Never assume that certain coworkers are shouldering office housework because they "enjoy" it or find it "rewarding."

Watch Your Words

As Security Nerdette pointed out in her Twitter thread, "How we spend our day is how we spend our life." It may seem like word choice is a minor issue, but it's one that accumulates over time.

- Be aware and respectful of pronouns and gendered language. Lead by example in how you use (or don't use) both.

- Create a safe space for people in your workplace or industry to ask questions and discuss problematic language.

- Be aware that some terms you think are innocuous may be harmful to others. If you mess up, apologize.

Share Speaking Opportunities

Allies who are truly dedicated to amplifying marginalized voices must be willing to give up a few choice speaking gigs so others may share their knowledge.

- If you are a man and are asked to speak as part of an all-male lineup, push back and/or decline.

- When you do present, ensure that your slide images show people from a variety of backgrounds, gender identities, and abilities.

- If you're offered a speaking engagement but know someone from an underrepresented group who could knock it out of the park, connect them to the event organizer and pass on the spot yourself.

Give Effective and Equitable Feedback

Feedback can be tricky to give, but it truly is a gift to receive. Without clear feedback, members of marginalized groups will have a much harder time succeeding and advancing. So, as an ally, remember:

- When giving feedback, focus on the business impact of an employee's work. What should they keep doing because it's moving the business forward? How should they improve in order to have an even bigger impact?

- Don't ease up just to avoid hurt feelings. Remember, vague feedback holds people back from growing in their careers.

- Tell them about the expertise you see in them and how to develop more job-related skills.

- Use objective criteria to evaluate employees in similar roles.

- Write reviews of the roughly the same length for everyone on your staff.

- Ask for feedback on how you can be a better ally.

Don't Be a Gatekeeper, Be a Door Opener

Helping people from underrepresented groups achieve their goals and advance their careers is one of the most powerful things allies can do. Here's how:

- Ask the people you manage or mentor about their career goals and, with permission, share them with influencers.

- Be equitable when handing out stretch assignments and other learning opportunities.

- Give wholehearted recommendations and referrals.

- Advocate effectively during performance calibration meetings and promotion discussions.

- Nudge colleagues from marginalized groups to pursue career growth opportunities.

- Sponsor people who are not like you. Speak their name when they aren't around. Endorse them publicly.

ACKNOWLEDGMENTS

Even for an introvert like me, the process of writing a book is a lonely one. It involves many solo hours working on the outline, repurposing blog posts, drafting new chapters, researching, and editing—all of which are engrossing and enriching activities but tough to do in total isolation. In fact, after a while I found myself battling with a serious case of impostor syndrome. The critic inside my head questioned if the book I was writing would be helpful to anyone, and fretted over relevant research or points of view I was forgetting to include.

So, like most authors, I sought out support and input, and received a boatload of insight and reassurance. While what I've written is far from comprehensive, I do hope *Better Allies* is helpful to all who read it. And I want to thank all those who helped me make it happen.

First of all, a huge thank you to Tim and our children Emma and Ted. Not only did you cheer me on every step of the way, you also helped me brainstorm ideas, reviewed drafts, and proofread every word. This book was definitely a family effort!

I also want to thank Cate Huston, my collaborator on the bingo card that started it all. Would this book have come about if we hadn't first created that card and its diversity-driven affirmations for allies? I don't think so.

To my myriad supporters on social media, I'm forever grateful. Through your engagement with my handle @betterallies, I discovered which points resonated and I refined how I wanted to talk about allyship. With your positive reinforcement and invaluable insights, I developed my voice and found the courage to write this book.

I'm also grateful to every single person who shared a story with me. I wanted this book to include a multitude of perspectives and voices, and it is so much better as a result of your contributions.

To the reviewers who provided me with invaluable feedback on my manuscript (especially Norm and Joe) and those who wrote testimonials to help me spread the word about my book, many thanks!

And to Susan Fowler, whose blog post in February 2017 catalyzed conversations about the lack of inclusive cultures across tech, a heartfelt thank-you. You paved the way for authors like me.

Last but not least, to my writing partner, Sally McGraw: I couldn't have done it without you. Thank you so very much.

ADDITIONAL RESOURCES

Books on Inclusion

Athena Rising: How and Why Men Should Mentor Women by W. Brad Johnson, PhD and David Smith, PhD, 2016

Inclusion: Diversity, The New Workplace, and The Will To Change by Jennifer Brown, 2017

One: How Male Allies Support Women For Gender Equality by Julie Kratz, 2017

White Fragility: Why It's So Hard For White People To Talk About Racism by Robin DiAngelo, 2018

Whistling Vivaldi: How Stereotypes Affect Us and What We Can Do by Claude M. Steele, 2011

Inclusion and Diversity Websites

Catalyst: www.catalyst.org

Corner of the Court: www.cornerofthecourt.com

Job Accommodation Network: www.askjan.org

The Leaky Tech Pipeline, Kapor Center: www.leakytechpipeline.com

National Center for Transgender Equality: www.transequality.org

National Center for Women in Information Technology (NCWIT): www.ncwit.org

Project Implicit: implicit.harvard.edu

Project Include: www.projectinclude.org

Stock Photography Featuring Underrepresented Minorities

CreateHER Stock: createherstock.com
Images featuring women of color. Some free, some available for a fee.

Jopwell Collection: jopwellcollection.jopwell.com
Free stock photos featuring Black, Latino/Hispanic, and Native American professionals.

Lean In Collection at Getty Images:
www.gettyimages.com/collections/leanin
Images devoted to the powerful depiction of women, girls and the people who support them. Available for a fee.

PhotoAbility: photoability.net
Images of people with differing abilities, available for a fee.

TONL: tonl.co
Diverse stock photos, available for a fee.

UKBlackTech: ukblacktech.com/stockphotos
Free stock photos of Black, Asian and minority ethnics using technology.

WOCintechchat: www.flickr.com/photos/wocintechchat
Free stock photos of women of color working in tech settings.

Videos

"3 ways to be a better ally in the workplace" by Melinda Epler at TED Salon,
www.ted.com/talks/melinda_epler_3_ways_to_advocate_for _a_more_inclusive_workplace

"Are you biased? I am" by Kristen Pressner at TEDxBasel, www.youtube.com/watch?v=Bq_xYSOZrgU

"The urgency of intersectionality" by Kimberlé Crenshaw at TEDWomen,
www.ted.com/talks/kimberle_crenshaw_the_urgency_of_int
ersectionality

Articles on Using More Inclusive Language

"100 Ways to Make the World Better for Non-binary People" by AC Dumlao.
broadly.vice.com/en_us/article/evkwm4/how-to-be-an-ally-
to-non-binary-gender-non-conforming-people-support

"The Radical Copyeditor's Style Guide for Writing About Transgender People" by Alex Kapitan.
radicalcopyeditor.com/2017/08/31/transgender-style-guide/

"70 Inclusive Language Principles That Will Make You A More Successful Recruiter" by Nehemiah Green.
medium.com/diversity-together/70-inclusive-language-
principles-that-will-make-you-a-more-successful-recruiter-
part-1-79b7342a0923

Source for an Inclusive Language Slackbot

www.betterallies.com/language/

ABOUT THE AUTHOR

Karen Catlin is a leadership coach, keynote speaker, author, and passionate advocate for inclusion in the workplace. After spending twenty-five years building software products and serving as a vice president of engineering at Macromedia and Adobe, she witnessed a sharp decline in the number of women working in tech. Frustrated but galvanized, she knew it was time to switch gears.

Today, Karen coaches women to be stronger leaders and men to be better allies. Her client roster includes Airbnb, Pinterest, eBay, and Intel, as well as a variety of motivated entrepreneurs and individuals. Karen's coaching offerings include tactics for increasing visibility, being more strategic, managing stakeholders, negotiation, and cultivating ally skills. Her writing on these and related topics has appeared in *Inc.*, the *Daily Beast*, and *Fast Company*, and she's consulted on articles for the *Wall Street Journal*, *Forbes*, and the *New York Times*. In late 2014, Karen started the Twitter handle @betterallies to share simple, actionable steps that anyone could take to make their workplaces more inclusive. She continues to tweet and blog for Better Allies, and also emails a roundup of "5 Ally Actions" to her subscribers every week.

A self-professed public speaking geek, Karen is a highly sought-after and engaging presenter who has delivered talks at more than a hundred conferences and corporate events. She speaks on a variety of topics, including inclusive workplaces and women in leadership. Her TEDx talk, "Women in Tech: The Missing Force," explores the decline in gender diversity in tech, why it's a problem, and what can be done about it. In addition to speaking herself, Karen is determined to change the ratio for who is on stage giving keynotes and other presentations. To support her goal of bringing more diversity to speaker lineups at tech industry events, she coauthored the book *Present! A Techie's Guide to Public Speaking* with Poornima Vijayashanker.

Karen is a graduate and active alum of Brown University, serving as an advisor to the university's Computer Science Diversity Initiative and mentoring students on how to launch their careers. She's also on the advisory boards for the Women's CLUB of Silicon Valley and WEST (Women Entering and Staying in Technology). In 2015, the California State Assembly honored Karen with the Wonder Women Tech Innovator Award for outstanding achievements in business and technology and for being a role model for women.

Karen and her partner Tim live in San Mateo, California. They're the proud parents of two Gen Z children, Emma and Ted.

To find out what Karen's up to next, visit her website at karencatlin.com.

NOTES

Introduction

1 "Gender Diversity Is a Competitive Advantage," Morgan Stanley, May 12, 2016, https://www.morganstanley.com/blog/women/gender-diversity-work.

2 Selena Larson, "Microsoft CEO Satya Nadella to Women: Don't Ask for a Raise, Trust Karma," *ReadWrite*, October 9, 2014, https://readwrite.com/2014/10/09/nadella-women-dont-ask-for-raise/.

3 Tanya Tarr, "By the Numbers: What Pay Inequality Looks Like for Women in Tech," *Forbes*, April 4, 2018, https://www.forbes.com/sites/tanyatarr/2018/04/04/by-the-numbers-what-pay-inequality-looks-like-for-women-in-tech/#2a7fbab860b1.

4 Selena Larson, "White Male 'Allies' Have Surprisingly Little to Say about Fixing Sexist Tech Culture," *ReadWrite*, October 9, 2014, https://readwrite.com/2014/10/09/technology-sexism-male-allies-grace-hopper-celebration/.

5 Buck Gee and Denise Peck, *The Illusion of Asian Success: Scant Progress for Minorities in Cracking the Glass Ceiling from 2007–2015* (New York: Ascend, 2017), https://c.ymcdn.com/sites/www.ascendleadership.org/resource/resmgr/research/TheIllusionofAsianSuccess.pdf.

6 Rani Molla, "It's Not Just Google—Many Major Tech Companies Are Struggling with Diversity," *Recode*, August 7, 2017, https://www.recode.net/2017/8/7/16108122/major-tech-companies-silicon-valley-diversity-women-tech-engineer.

7 Sam Levin, "What Happens When Tech Firms End Up at the Center of Racism Scandals?" *The Guardian*, August 30, 2016, https://www.theguardian.com/technology/2016/aug/30/tech-companies-racial-discrimination-nextdoor-airbnb.

Chapter 1

8   "What Is Intersectionality?" Grinnell College, accessed October 1, 2018, http://haenfler.sites.grinnell.edu/subcultural-theory-and-theorists/intersectionality/.

9   Kittu Pannu, "Privilege, Power, and Pride: Intersectionality Within the LGBT Community," *Impakter*, August 14, 2017, https://impakter.com/privilege-power-and-pride-intersectionality-within-the-lgbt-community/.

10 Kimberlé Crenshaw, "The Urgency of Intersectionality," filmed October 2016, TED video, 18:50, https://www.ted.com/talks/kimberle_crenshaw_the_urgency_of_intersectionality.

11 Sian Ferguson, "Privilege 101: A Quick and Dirty Guide," *Everyday Feminism*, September 29, 2014, https://everydayfeminism.com/2014/09/what-is-privilege/.

12 Icons in this section are from the "Noun Project" (https://thenounproject.com) by Adrien Coquet, Dinosoft Labs, unlimicon, Thomas' designs, ProSymbols, Ben Davis, and corpus delicti. Licensed under CC BY 3.0, https://creativecommons.org/licenses/by/3.0/.

13 Andrew Grill, "I Gave Up My Seat at an All-Male Panel to a Woman—And More Men Should Do the Same," *Huffington Post*, May 27, 2015, https://www.huffingtonpost.com/andrew-grill/i-gave-up-my-seat-at-an-all-male-panel-to-a-woman_b_7451512.html.

14 Susan Wojcicki, "Exclusive: How to Break Up the Silcon Valley Boys' Club," *Vanity Fair*, March 16, 2017, https://www.vanityfair.com/news/2017/03/how-to-break-up-the-silicon-valley-boys-club-susan-wojcicki.

Chapter 2

15 Better Male Allies, "Male Allies: The Tech Industry Needs You," Opensource.com, June 13, 2017, https://opensource.com/article/17/6/male-allies-tech-industry-needs-you.

16 Jason van Gumster, "Haters Gonna Hate: 7 Ways to Deal with Criticism," Opensource.com, April 27, 2017, https://opensource.com/article/17/4/haters-gonna-hate.

17 Craig Froehle, "The Evolution of an Accidental Meme," *Medium*,
    April 14, 2016, https://medium.com/@CRA1G/the-evolution-of-
    an-accidental-meme-ddc4e139e0e4.

Chapter 3

18 "Discussing Discrimination," American Psychological Association,
    accessed October 1, 2018, http://www.apa.org/helpcenter/keita-
    qa.aspx.

19 Dwight Smith, "The 8 R's of Talking about Race: How to Have
    Meaningful Conversations," *Net Impact*, June 18, 2015,
    https://www.netimpact.org/blog/the-8-r%E2%80%99s-of-talking-
    about-race-how-to-have-meaningful-conversations.

20 "Discussing Discrimination," American Psychological Association.

21 "Ten Lessons for Talking about Race, Racism and Racial Justice,"
    The Opportunity Agenda, February 23, 2017,
    https://opportunityagenda.org/explore/resources-publications/ten-
    lessons-talking-about-race-racism-and-racial-justice.

22 Robin DiAngelo, "How White People Handle Diversity Training in
    the Workplace," *Medium*, June 27, 2018,
    https://medium.com/s/story/how-white-people-handle-diversity-
    training-in-the-workplace-e8408d2519f.

23 Annalee Flower Horne, "How 'Good Intent' Undermines Diversity
    and Inclusion," *The Bias*, September 26, 2017,
    https://thebias.com/2017/09/26/how-good-intent-undermines-
    diversity-and-inclusion/.

24 Arianna O'Dell, "Dear Blockchain Bros, I Won't Let Your Sexism
    Poison Our Industry," *Fast Company*, April 11, 2018,
    https://www.fastcompany.com/40556187/dear-blockchain-bros-i-
    wont-let-your-sexism-poison-our-industry.

25 Laura Vitto, "#MeToo's Tarana Burke Calls Out Tony Robbins for
    His Tone-Deaf Comments," April 7, 2018, *Mashable*,
    https://mashable.com/2018/04/07/tony-robbins-me-too-
    comments-tamara-burke/#o8TMztKwQiqB.

26 "Six Steps to Speak Up," Teaching Tolerance, 2005,
    https://www.tolerance.org/magazine/publications/speak-up/six-
    steps-to-speak-up.

27   "Six Steps to Speak Up," Teaching Tolerance.

28   Farhad Manjoo, "Ellen Pao Disrupts How Silicon Valley Does Business," *New York Times*, March 27, 2015, https://www.nytimes.com/2015/03/28/technology/ellen-pao-disrupts-how-silicon-valley-does-business.html.

Chapter 4

29   Allison Scott, Freada Kapor Klein, Frieda McAlear, Alexis Martin, and Sonia Koshy, *The Leaky Tech Pipeline: A Comprehensive Framework for Understanding and Addressing the Lack of Diversity across the Tech Ecosystem* (Oakland, CA: Kapor Center for Social Impact, February 2018), http://www.leakytechpipeline.com/wp-content/themes/kapor/pdf/KC18001_report_v6.pdf.

30   Rachel Thomas, Marianne Cooper, Ellen Konar, Megan Rooney, Ashley Finch, Lareina Yee, Alexis Krivkovich, Irina Starikova, Kelsey Robinson, and Rachel Valentino, *Women in the Workplace 2017* (New York and Palo Alto, CA: McKinsey & Company and LeanIn.Org, 2017), https://womenintheworkplace.com/2017.

31   Devon Magliozzi, "Building Effective Networks: Nurturing Strategic Relationships, Especially for Women," The Clayman Institute for Gender Research, April 26, 2016, https://gender.stanford.edu/news-publications/gender-news/building-effective-networks-nurturing-strategic-relationships.

32   Drake Baer, "Why You Need a Diverse Network," August 13, 2013, *Fast Company*, https://www.fastcompany.com/3015552/why-you-need-a-diverse-network.

33   Ivan Misner, "The Importance of Diversity in Networking," *Entrepreneur*, January 26, 2004, https://www.entrepreneur.com/article/68840.

34   Paul Gompers and Silpa Kovvali, "The Other Diversity Dividend," *Harvard Business Review*, July 2018, https://hbr.org/2018/07/the-other-diversity-dividend.

35   "Men, Commit to Mentor Women," LeanIn.Org, accessed February 9, 2018, https://leanin.org/mentor-her.

36   "Men, Commit to Mentor Women," LeanIn.Org.

37   Nikki Graf, "Sexual Harassment at Work in the Era of #MeToo,"
     Pew Research Center, April 4, 2018,
     http://www.pewsocialtrends.org/2018/04/04/sexual-harassment-at-
     work-in-the-era-of-metoo/.

38   Harris O'Malley, "Treating Men like Idiots Is the Wrong Way to Stop
     Sexual Harassment," *Washington Post*, February 1, 2018,
     https://www.washingtonpost.com/news/post-
     nation/wp/2018/02/01/for-men-in-the-metoo-era-the-mike-pence-
     rule-is-the-easy-way-out/.

39   "Men, Commit to Mentor Women," LeanIn.Org.

40   Caroline Kitchener, "When It's Hard for Women to Find Male
     Mentors," *The Atlantic*, August 22, 2017,
     https://www.theatlantic.com/business/archive/2017/08/women-
     men-mentorship/537201/.

41   Rachel Thomas, Marianne Cooper, Ellen Konar, Megan Rooney,
     Mary Noble-Tolla, Ali Bohrer, Lareina Yee, et al., *Women in the
     Workplace 2018* (New York and Palo Alto, CA: McKinsey &
     Company and LeanIn.Org, 2018), accessed November 1, 2018,
     https://womenintheworkplace.com.

Chapter 5

42   Derald Wing Sue, "Microaggressions: More Than Just Race,"
     Psychology Today, November 17, 2010,
     https://www.psychologytoday.com/us/blog/microaggressions-in-
     everyday-life/201011/microaggressions-more-just-race.

43   Rachel Premack, "9 Things People Think Are Fine to Say at Work—
     but Are Actually Racist, Sexist, or Offensive," *Business Insider*, July 3,
     2018, https://www.businessinsider.com/microaggression-
     unconscious-bias-at-work-2018-6.

44   Theodore Henderson, "How Good Leadership Can Minimize
     Microaggressions," *Forbes*, March 7, 2017,
     https://www.forbes.com/sites/forbescoachescouncil/2017/03/07/
     how-good-leadership-can-minimize-
     microaggressions/#6b8e19594d70.

45   ADA National Network, *A Planning Guide for Making Temporary Events
     Accessible to People with Disabilities*, 2015,
     https://adata.org/publication/temporary-events-guide.

46   Kara Sowles, "Alchol and Inclusivity,"
     https://docs.google.com/presentation/d/e/2PACX-
     1vSyiiMJH68OF3BT1w6vqwawHyKEGNF5TTbR1cUf7FWXYadR
     mZpi9wvv0k-O7glfbhVX0rC7kGIzgKzk/pub?slide=id.p.

47   Justin Murphy, "Risque Photos Cause Controversy at Turtle and Fish
     Conference," *Democrat and Chronicle*, July 13, 2018,
     https://www.democratandchronicle.com/story/news/2018/07/13/
     metoo-jmih-dick-vogt-rochester-herpetologist/782002002/.

48   "Our Commitment to Our Community," Mapbox, accessed
     November 1, 2018, https://www.mapbox.com/events/code-of-
     conduct/. Creative Commons Attribution-ShareAlike 4.0
     International (CC BY-SA 4.0) license. Reformatted in publishing.

49   Valerie Aurora, *Code of Conduct Training* (San Francisco: Frame Shift
     Consulting, n.d.),
     https://files.frameshiftconsulting.com/codeofconducttraining.pdf

50   Aurora, *Code of Conduct Training*.

Chapter 6

51   Sohan Murthy, "Measuring Gender Diversity with Data from
     LinkedIn," *LinkedIn Official Blog*, June 17, 2015,
     https://blog.linkedin.com/2015/06/17/measuring-gender-diversity-
     with-data-from-linkedin.

52   Joelle Emerson, "Want to Hire More a More Diverse Set of People?
     Raise Your Bar." *Medium*, May 11, 2015,
     https://medium.com/inclusion-insights/want-to-hire-more-diverse-
     people-raise-your-bar-b5d30f91cbd9.

53   Jessi Hempel, "Why Are There Few Women in Tech? Watch a
     Recruiting Session," *Wired*, March 1, 2018,
     https://www.wired.com/story/why-are-there-few-women-in-tech-
     watch-a-recruiting-session/.

54   Makinde Adeagbo, "Racial Fault Lines in Silicon Valley," *Medium*,
     May 25, 2016, https://blog.devcolor.org/racial-fault-lines-in-silicon-
     valley-390cd0e4a6dc.

55   "Top 10 Ways to Hire the Best for Your Computing Start-Up,"
     National Center for Women in Information Technology, accessed
     September 29, 2018, https://www.ncwit.org/resources/top-10-ways-
     hire-best-your-computing-start/top-10-ways-hire-best-your-
     computing-start.

56   Entertainment Software Association, *2014 Essential Facts about the
     Computer and Video Game Industry*, 2014, http://www.theesa.com/wp-
     content/uploads/2014/10/ESA_EF_2014.pdf; Audrey L. Brehm,
     "Navigating the Feminine in Massively Multiplayer Online Games:
     Gender in World of Warcraft," *Frontiers in Psychology* 4 (2013): 903,
     https://doi.org/10.3389/fpsyg.2013.00903.

57   Change.org careers page, accessed July 31, 2014,
     https://www.change.org/careers.

58   "Who Are the Caregivers?" Family Caregiving Alliance, December
     31, 2003, https://www.caregiver.org/women-and-caregiving-facts-
     and-figures.

59   "Supervising-in-a-Box Series: Employee Recruitment/Selection,"
     National Center for Women in Information Technology, February
     12, 2010, https://www.ncwit.org/resources/supervising-box-series-
     employee-recruitmentselection.

60   Danielle Gaucher, Justin Friesen, and Aaron C. Kay, "Evidence That
     Gendered Wording in Job Advertisements Exists and Sustains
     Gender Inequality," *Journal of Personality and Social Psychology* 101, no. 1
     (July 2011): 109–28, https://doi.org/10.1037/a0022530.

61   Tech Companies That Only Hire Men (website), accessed August 18 ,
     2018, http://techcompaniesthatonlyhiremen.tumblr.com/.

62   Original study unavailable. See summaries in: Sheryl Sandberg, *Lean
     In: Women, Work, and the Will to Lead*, with Nell Scovell (New York:
     Alfred A. Knopf, 2013); Katty Kay and Claire Shipman, *The Confidence
     Code: The Science and Art of Self-Assurance—What Women Should Know*
     (New York: HarperCollins, 2014).

63   Jo Owen, *How to Lead* (Upper Saddle River, NJ: Prentice Hall, 2011).

64   Tara Sophia Mohr, "Why Women Don't Apply for Jobs Unless
     They're 100% Qualified," *Harvard Business Review*, August 25, 2014,
     https://hbr.org/2014/08/why-women-dont-apply-for-jobs-unless-
     theyre-100-qualified.

65 Klint Finley, "Diversity in Open Source Is Even Worse Than in Tech Overall," *Wired*, June 2, 2017, https://www.wired.com/2017/06/diversity-open-source-even-worse-tech-overall/.

66 Kendall Tucker, "Tips for Hiring Women in Tech from a Female Ceo Who Had Trouble Hiring Women in Tech," W2.0, July 17, 2018, http://www.women2.com/2018/07/17/tips-for-hiring-women-in-tech-from-a-female-ceo-who-had-trouble-hiring-women-in-tech/.

67 Abby Madonado, "Diversifying Engineering Referrals at Pinterest," LinkedIn, January 15, 2016, https://www.linkedin.com/pulse/diversifying-engineering-referrals-pinterest-abby-maldonado/.

68 Kenneth Johnson, "What Corporations Can Learn about Diversity from the NFL's Rooney Rule," *Forbes*, February 1, 2018, https://www.forbes.com/sites/forbescoachescouncil/2018/02/01/what-corporations-can-learn-about-diversity-from-the-nfls-rooney-rule/#360cd19347de.

69 Jethro Nededog, "J.J. Abrams Believes Diversity Is Good for Business—and He's Taking One Big Step to Prove It," *Business Insider*, March 2, 2016, https://www.businessinsider.com/jj-abrams-diversity-policy-2016-3.

70 Christina Passariello, "Tech Firms Borrow Football Play to Increase Hiring of Women," *Wall Street Journal*, September 27, 2016, https://www.wsj.com/articles/tech-firms-borrow-football-play-to-increase-hiring-of-women-1474963562.

71 "Tech Workforce Barriers," Kapor Center for Social Impact, accessed November 1, 2018, http://www.leakytechpipeline.com/barrier/tech-workforce-barriers/.

72 Lauren A. Rivera, "Guess Who Doesn't Fit In at Work," *New York Times*, May 30, 2015, https://www.nytimes.com/2015/05/31/opinion/sunday/guess-who-doesnt-fit-in-at-work.html.

73 Textio, "Webinar: How to Fight Diversity Fatigue," Vimeo video, May 14, 2018, 56:24, https://vimeo.com/269693446/624660f941.

74 Lydia Dishman, "How Google, Pinterest, and Others Use Internships to Push Their Diversity Initiatives," *Fast Company*, May 23, 2016, https://www.fastcompany.com/3060118/how-google-pinterest-and-others-use-internships-to-push-their-diversity-i.

75 Iris Bohnet, "How to Take the Bias out of Interviews," *Harvard Business Review*, April 18, 2016, https://hbr.org/2016/04/how-to-take-the-bias-out-of-interviews.

76 Laszlo Bock, "Here's Google's Secret to Hiring the Best People," *Wired*, April 7, 2015, https://www.wired.com/2015/04/hire-like-google/.

77 Project Implicit (website), accessed November 1, 2018, https://implicit.harvard.edu.

78 Jason Wong, "Inclusion Interviewing," *Jason Wong's Blog*, July 2, 2018, https://www.attack-gecko.net/2018/07/02/inclusion-interviewing/.

79 Laszlo Bock, *Work Rules! Insights from inside Google That Will Transform How You Live and Lead* (New York: Twelve Books, 2015).

80 Lindsay Gellman and Georgia Wells, "What's Holding Back Women in Tech?" *Wall Street Journal*, March 22, 2016, https://www.wsj.com/articles/whats-holding-back-women-in-tech-1458639004.

81 The Leaky Tech Pipeline (website), Kapor Center for Social Impact, http://www.leakytechpipeline.com/.

82 "Programs & Initiatives," The Leaky Tech Pipeline, accessed November 1, 2018, http://www.leakytechpipeline.com/featured-programs/tech-workforce/.

83 Larissa Shapiro, personal communication, September 20, 2018.

Chapter 7

84 Claire Zillman, "Ruth Bader Ginsburg Used This Simple Trick to Cut Down on 'Manterrupting'," *Fortune*, April 6, 2017, http://fortune.com/2017/04/06/ruth-bader-ginsburg-supreme-court-advice-interrupting/.

85 Deborah Tannen, "The Truth about How Much Women Talk—and Whether Men Listen," *Time*, June 28, 2017, http://time.com/4837536/do-women-really-talk-more/.

86   "Crowd Erupts at World Science Festival after Moderator Is Called Out for 'Mansplaining,'" Women in the World, June 9, 2017, https://womenintheworld.com/2017/06/09/crowd-erupts-at-world-science-festival-after-moderator-is-called-out-for-mansplaining/.

87   "Meeting Skills," Frame Shift Consulting, accessed September 1, 2018, https://frameshiftconsulting.com/meeting-skills/.

88   Claire Landsbaum, "Obama's Female Staffers Came Up with a Genius Strategy to Make Sure Their Voices Were Heard," *The Cut*, September 13, 2016, https://www.thecut.com/2016/09/heres-how-obamas-female-staffers-made-their-voices-heard.html.

89   Molly Peeples (@astronomolly), "Meeting scene this morning," Twitter, July 18, 2018, 11:24 a.m., https://twitter.com/astronomolly/status/1019618860616568833.

90   Helaine Olen, "Alexandria Ocasio-Cortez Is Not Your Manic Pixie Dream Girl," *Washington Post*, August 10, 2018, https://www.washingtonpost.com/blogs/post-partisan/wp/2018/08/10/alexandria-ocasio-cortez-is-not-your-manic-pixie-dream-girl/.

91   Hilary Jerome Scarsella, "Story time. I'm at the airport, working on my laptop, sitting near a guy I just met at a conference this weekend," Facebook, September 22, 2018, https://www.facebook.com/hilary.scarsella/posts/10111805198524389.

92   Elephant in the Valley, accessed June 1, 2018, https://www.elephantinthevalley.com/.

93   Elizabeth Giorgi, personal communication, October 14, 2018.

Chapter 8

94   Elephant in the Valley.

95   Linda Babcock, Maria P. Recalde, and Lise Vesterlund, "Why Women Volunteer for Tasks That Don't Lead to Promotions," *Harvard Business Review*, July 16, 2018, https://hbr.org/2018/07/why-women-volunteer-for-tasks-that-dont-lead-to-promotions.

96 Ruchika Tulshyan, "Women of Color Get Asked to Do More 'Office Housework.' Here's How They Can Say No," *Harvard Business Review*, April 6, 2018, https://hbr.org/2018/04/women-of-color-get-asked-to-do-more-office-housework-heres-how-they-can-say-no.

97 Tulshyan, "Women of Color Get Asked to Do More 'Office Housework.'"

98 Richard Branson, "Take Note, It's Time to Take Notes," Virgin, February 12, 2015, https://www.virgin.com/richard-branson/take-note-its-time-to-take-notes.

99 Branson, "Take Note, It's Time to Take Notes."

100 Joan C. Williams, "Sticking Women with the Office Housework," *Washington Post*, April 16, 2014, https://www.washingtonpost.com/news/on-leadership/wp/2014/04/16/sticking-women-with-the-office-housework/.

101 Tulshyan, "Women of Color Get Asked to Do More 'Office Housework.'"

Chapter 9

102 Deb Liu, "The Right Words for the Job: How Gendered Language Affects the Workplace," *Medium*, February 25, 2017, https://medium.com/women-in-product/genderwords-b0be0cc8251f.

103 Kim Z. Dale, "40 Gender-Neutral Alternatives to Saying 'You Guys,'" ChicagoNow, May 24, 2017, http://www.chicagonow.com/listing-beyond-forty/2017/05/40-gender-neutral-alternatives-to-saying-you-guys/.

104 Amanda Prestigiacomo, "London Tube Just Banned the Phrase 'Ladies and Gentlemen' to Be More 'Inclusive,'" *The Daily Wire*, July 14, 2017, https://www.dailywire.com/news/18600/london-tube-just-banned-innocuous-phrase-be-more-amanda-prestigiacomo.

105 Clár McWeeney, "Let's Talk about the Word 'Lady,'" *Clue*, September 6, 2017, https://helloclue.com/articles/culture/lets-talk-about-word-lady.

106 *Merriam-Webster*, s.v. "they (*pro.*)," accessed November 1, 2018, https://www.merriam-webster.com/dictionary/they.

107 Jessi Elana Aaron, "'Lame,' 'Stand Up' and Other Words We Use to Insult the Disabled without Even Knowing It," *Washington Post*, May 13, 2015, https://www.washingtonpost.com/posteverything/wp/2015/05/13/lame-stand-up-and-other-words-we-use-to-insult-the-disabled-without-even-knowing-it/.

108 Rachel Cohen-Rottenberg, "Doing Social Justice: Thoughts on Ableist Language and Why It Matters," Disability and Representation, September 14, 2013, www.disabilityandrepresentation.com/2013/09/14/ableist-language/.

109 Lydia X. Z. Brown, "Ableism/Language," Autistic Hoya, last updated December 7, 2016), www.autistichoya.com/p/ableist-words-and-terms-to-avoid.html.

110 Paul Gowder, "What Is a Native American Pow Wow," PowWows.com, July 24, 2011, https://www.powwows.com/what-is-a-pow-wow/.

111 Michelle Glauser (@MichelleGlauser), "To avoid being disrespectful by using the word 'powwow,' you can use words such as 'meeting,' 'check-in,' 'stand-up,' 'talk,' 'huddle,' 'one-on-one.'" Twitter, August 30, 2018, 1:52 p.m., https://twitter.com/MichelleGlauser/status/1035238798945181697.

112 "Use These Culturally Offensive Phrases, Questions at Your Own Risk," Indigenous Corporate Training Inc., September 22, 2015, https://www.ictinc.ca/blog/culturally-offensive-phrases-you-should-use-at.

113 Security Nerdette (@secnerdette), "Replacing 'whitelist/blacklist' with 'safelist/blocklist' now on," Twitter, August 17, 2017, 5:42 p.m., https://twitter.com/secnerdette/status/898314208097427457.

114 Bron Lewis, "Language Matters," *Nuna*, May 10, 2018, https://blog.nuna.com/language-matters-7fced5d78f8d.

115 Jensen Moore (@MagicalPR), "Added Dr. to my Twitter name today," Twitter, June 17, 2018, 8:41 a.m., https://twitter.com/MagicalPR/status/1008343920269496322.

116 Marisa Franco (@MarisaGFranco), "Tip: Instead of asking unfamiliar faces in your department 'are you a student?' ask 'what is your role, here?'" Twitter, August 14, 2018, 11:14 a.m., https://twitter.com/MarisaGFranco/status/1029400971355582464.

117 Suzanne Wertheim (@WorthwhileRandC), "It's one of the most basic ways to avoid giving an unconscious demotion," Twitter, August 15, 2018, 1:05 p.m., https://twitter.com/WorthwhileRandC/status/1029791229624479744.

118 Security Nerdette (@secnerdette), "I used to think the same way!" Twitter, August 17, 2017, 6:13 p.m., https://twitter.com/secnerdette/status/898321808889266176.

Chapter 10

119 AnitaB.org, "Megan Smith - Importance of Diverse Ideas in Gov't GHC15," YouTube video, November 30, 2015, 23:19, https://www.youtube.com/watch?v=ILzUpCA_ozE.

120 Richard Bradshaw, "My Speaker Rider and Why It's Needed," Friendly Tester, June 12, 2018, https://thefriendlytester.co.uk/2018/06/my-speaker-rider-and-why.

121 Adam Singer (@AdamSinger), "Yo, fellow guys in tech," Twitter, January 29, 2018, 11:23 a.m., https://twitter.com/AdamSinger/status/958027769429950464.

122 Matt May (@mattmay), "If someone hands you a microphone at a conference Q&A," Twitter, October 3, 2018, 1:27 p.m., https://twitter.com/mattmay/status/1047553774884020224.

123 Pluralsight, "Pluralsight LIVE 2017 Mainstage: Joel Spolsky, CEO, Stack Overflow," YouTube video, October 4, 2017, 21:59, www.youtube.com/watch?v=5OJIVp1CgFY.

Chapter 11

124 Shelley Correll and Caroline Simard, "Research: Vague Feedback Is Holding Women Back," Harvard Business Review, April 29, 2016, https://hbr.org/2016/04/research-vague-feedback-is-holding-women-back.

125 Kieran Snyder, "The Abrasiveness Trap: High-Achieving Men and Women Are Described Differently in Reviews," *Fortune*, August 26, 2014, http://fortune.com/2014/08/26/performance-review-gender-bias/.

126 Correll and Simard, "Research: Vague Feedback Is Holding Women Back."

127 Gillian B. White, "Black Workers Really Do Need to Be Twice as Good," *The Atlantic*, October 7, 2015, https://www.theatlantic.com/business/archive/2015/10/why-black-workers-really-do-need-to-be-twice-as-good/409276/.

128 National Public Radio, Robert Wood Johnson Foundation, and Harvard T.H. Chan School of Public Health, *Discrimination in America: Experiences and Views of LGBTQ Americans*, November 2017, https://www.rwjf.org/content/dam/farm/reports/surveys_and_poll s/2017/rwjf441734, 1.

129 Sandy E. James, Jody L. Herman, Susan Rankin, Mara Keisling, Lisa Mottet, and Ma'ayan Anafi, *The Report of the 2015 U.S. Transgender Survey* (Washington: National Center for Transgender Equality, 2016), https://transequality.org/sites/default/files/docs/usts/USTS-Full-Report-Dec17.pdf, 148.

130 David G. Smith, Judith E. Rosenstein, and Margaret C. Nikolov, "How Performance Evaluations Hurt Gender Equality," *Behavioral Scientist*, June 26, 2018, http://behavioralscientist.org/how-performance-evaluations-hurt-gender-equality/.

131 Jean Martin, "A Fairer Way to Make Hiring and Promotion Decisions," *Harvard Business Review*, August 13, 2013, https://hbr.org/2013/08/a-fairer-way-to-make-hiring-an.

132 Smith, Rosenstein, and Nikolov, "How Performance Evaluations Hurt Gender Equality."

133 Anna Gifty (@itsafronomics), "So.. today, a professor questioned whether I could pursue a PhD in economics," Twitter, September 5, 2018, 7:27 p.m., https://twitter.com/itsafronomics/status/1037497390859776000.

134 Patty Lopez (@pittrpatt), "When I see someone who I don't know at an event, I assume they belong and introduce myself," Twitter, September 7, 2018, 3:09 p.m., https://twitter.com/pittrpatt/status/1038157229705310209.

135 Mikki Hebl, Christine L. Nittrouer, Abigail R. Corrington, and Juan M. Madera, "How We Describe Male and Female Job Applicants Differently," *Harvard Business Review*, September 27, 2018, https://hbr.org/2018/09/how-we-describe-male-and-female-job-applicants-differently.

136 TEDx Talks, "Are You Biased? I Am | Kristen Pressner | TEDxBasel," YouTube video, August 20, 2016, 8:48, https://www.youtube.com/watch?v=Bq_xYSOZrgU.

137 "The Leaky Tech Pipeline," Kapor Center for Social Impact, accessed November 1, 2018, http://www.leakytechpipeline.com/.

138 Elise Gould, *The State of American Wages 2017* (Washington: Economic Policy Institute, March 2018), https://www.epi.org/publication/the-state-of-american-wages-2017-wages-have-finally-recovered-from-the-blow-of-the-great-recession-but-are-still-growing-too-slowly-and-unequally/.

139 P.R. Lockhart, "Tuesday is Black Women's Equal Pay Day. Here's what you should know about the gap," Vox, Aug 7, 2018, https://www.vox.com/identities/2018/8/7/17657416/black-womens-equal-pay-day-gender-racial-pay-gap.

140 "The Leaky Tech Pipeline," Kapor Center for Social Impact.

141 Derek Miller, "Occupations with the Largest and Smallest Pay Gap – 2018 Edition," Smart Asset, September 20, 2018, https://smartasset.com/retirement/largest-and-smallest-pay-gap-occupations-2018-edition.

142 Miller, "Occupations with the Largest and Smallest Pay Gap – 2018 Edition."

143 Marcel Schwantes, "The CEO of Salesforce Found Out His Female Employees Were Paid Less Than Men. His Response Is a Priceless Leadership Lesson," *Inc.*, July 26, 2018, https://www.inc.com/marcel-schwantes/the-ceo-of-salesforce-found-out-female-employees-are-paid-less-than-men-his-response-is-a-priceless-leadership-lesson.html.

144 Ivana Kottasová, "The Uk Has a Major Gender Pay Gap Problem. New Data Proves It," *CNN Business*, April 4, 2018, https://money.cnn.com/2018/04/03/news/economy/gender-pay-gap-deadline-uk/index.html.

145 Mani Rolla, "As Women in Tech Gain Experience, Their Pay Gap with Men Gets Worse," *Recode*, April 4, 2018, https://www.recode.net/2018/4/4/17188712/women-tech-salary-job-pay-gap-hired.

146 Benjamin Artz, Amanda Goodall, and Andrew J. Oswald, "Research: Women Ask for Raises as Often as Men, but Are Less Likely to Get Them," *Harvard Business Review*, June 25, 2018, https://hbr.org/2018/06/research-women-ask-for-raises-as-often-as-men-but-are-less-likely-to-get-them.

147 Lareina Yee, Alexis Krivkovich, Eric Kutcher, Blair Epstein, Rachel Thomas, Ashley Finch, Marianne Cooper, and Ellen Konar, *Women in the Workplace 2016* (Palo Alto, CA, and New York: LeanIn.Org and McKinsey & Company, 2017), https://womenintheworkplace.com/2016.

148 Kim Scott, *Radical Candor: Be a Kick-Ass Boss without Losing Your Humanity* (New York: St. Martin's Press, 2017), 153.

149 Correll and Simard, "Research: Vague Feedback Is Holding Women Back."

150 Chelsea Troy, "A Rubric for Evaluating Team Members' Contributions to an Inclusive Culture," May 24, 2018, https://chelseatroy.com/2018/05/24/why-your-efforts-to-make-your-company-inclusive-arent-working/.

Chapter 12

151 Oksana Malysheva, "Oksana's Story: Geoffrey Frost," The Corner of the Court Project, June 20, 2018, https://www.cornerofthecourt.com/oksanas-story-geoffrey-frost/.

152 Joan C. Williams and Marina Multhaup, "For Women and Minorities to Get Ahead, Managers Must Assign Work Fairly," *Harvard Business Review*, March 5, 2018, https://hbr.org/2018/03/for-women-and-minorities-to-get-ahead-managers-must-assign-work-fairly.

153 Dulini Fernando, Laurie Cohen, and Joanne Duberley, "What Managers Can Do to Keep Women in Engineering," *Harvard Business Review*, June 12, 2018, https://hbr.org/2018/06/what-managers-can-do-to-keep-women-in-engineering.

154 Nico Grant, "Big Tech, Little Diversity: Blacks Comprise 3% of Silicon Valley Talent," *Industry Week*, June 8, 2018, https://www.industryweek.com/technology-and-iiot/big-tech-little-diversity-blacks-comprise-3-silicon-valley-talent.

155 Melissa Locker, "Women of Color Are Less Likely to Get Patents for Their Work," *Fast Company*, July 24, 2018, https://www.fastcompany.com/90207134/women-of-color-are-less-likely-to-get-patents-for-their-work.

156 Catherine Ashcraft, "How Can Companies Promote Innovation with Diverse Employees?" National Center for Women and Information Technology, accessed March 1, 2014, https://www.ncwit.org/resources/how-can-companies-promote-innovation-diverse-employees/how-can-companies-promote.

157 Colleen Flaherty, "Help That Hurts Women," Inside Higher Ed, June 19, 2018, https://www.insidehighered.com/news/2018/06/19/study-finds-recommendation-letters-inadvertently-signal-doubt-about-female; Hebl et al., "How We Describe Male and Female Job Applicants Differently," September 27, 2018, Harvard Business Review, https://hbr.org/2018/09/how-we-describe-male-and-female-job-applicants-differently.

158 Tom Hartley (@tom_hartley), "Reading some of my draft references," Twitter, October 8, 2018, 6:22 a.m., https://twitter.com/tom_hartley/status/1049288840047984641.

159 Rosalind C. Barnett and Caryl Rivers, "How the 'New Discrimination' Is Holding Women Back," Catalyst, April 17, 2014, https://www.catalyst.org/zing/how-new-discrimination-holding-women-back.

160 Barnett and Rivers, "How the 'New Discrimination' Is Holding Women Back."

161 "Interrupting Bias in Performance Evaluations," Bias Interrupters, accessed November 1, 2018, https://biasinterrupters.org/interrupting-bias-in-performance-evaluations/.

162 Rachel Thomas, Marianne Cooper, Ellen Konar, Megan Rooney, Ashley Finch, Lareina Yee, Alexis Krivkovich, Irina Starikova, Kelsey Robinson, and Rachel Valentino, *Women in the Workplace 2017* (New York and Palo Alto, CA: McKinsey & Company and LeanIn.Org, 2017), https://womenintheworkplace.com/2017.

163 Tomas Chamorro-Premuzic, Seymour Adler, and Robert B. Kaiser. "What Science Says about Identifying High-Potential Employees," *Harvard Business Review*, October 3, 2017, https://hbr.org/2017/10/what-science-says-about-identifying-high-potential-employees.

164 Laszlo Bock, *Work Rules! Insights from Inside Google That Will Transform How You Live and Lead* (New York: Twelve Books, 2015).

165 Cecilia Kang, "Google Data-Mines Its Approach to Promoting Women," *Washington Post*, April 2, 2014, https://www.washingtonpost.com/news/the-switch/wp/2014/04/02/google-data-mines-its-women-problem/.

166 Freada Kapor Klein, "What's It Like to Be a Female Tech Entrepreneur?" *Medium*, September 14, 2018, https://medium.com/kapor-the-bridge/whats-it-like-to-be-a-female-tech-entrepreneur-a170a99089eb.

167 Sharethrough, "The Inclusive Leader - Developing Diverse Teams // Jill Wetzler // Calibrate 2017," YouTube video, November 10, 2017, 38:21, https://www.youtube.com/watch?v=PDepSAbhNuc.

Chapter 13

168 Matt Rosoff, "A Google Employee Posted a 10-Page Treatise about Bias, and People Are Outraged," CNBC, August 5, 2017, https://www.cnbc.com/2017/08/05/google-engineer-posts-anti-diversity-treatise.html.

169 Sophia Chen, "Physicists Condemn Sexism through 'Particles for Justice,'" *Wired*, October 5, 2018, https://www.wired.com/story/physicists-condemn-sexism-through-particles-for-justice/.

170 Katherine Long, "Why Don't Women Code? A UW Lecturer's Answer Draws Heat," *The Seattle Times*, June 22, 2018, https://www.seattletimes.com/seattle-news/education/why-dont-women-code-a-uw-lecturers-answer-draws-heat/.

171 Audrey Murrell, "On the Tennis Court and in the Workplace: When Unconscious Bias Isn't Unconscious," *Forbes*, September 20, 2018, https://www.forbes.com/sites/audreymurrell/2018/09/20/on-the-tennis-court-and-in-the-workplace-when-unconscious-bias-isnt-unconscious/.

172 Tom Peters (@tom_peters), "Bosses: Who are the four folks whose development path you will have dramatically effected by 12/31/18?" Twitter, December 29, 2017, 11:43 a.m., https://twitter.com/tom_peters/status/946783783835066368.

Bonus Chapter

173 Kristen Pressner, personal communication, April 23, 2018.

174 David Smith, personal communication, April 23, 2018.

175 Jennifer Brown, personal communication, April 24, 2018.

176 Cath Jones, personal communication, April 24, 2018.

Epilogue

177 Concerned Feminists (@concernedfems), "So this is happening. #ghc14 #ghcmanwatch," Twitter, October 8, 2014, 8:31 p.m., https://twitter.com/concernedfems/status/520023816769388547.

178 Cate Huston and Karen Catlin, "Tech's Male 'Feminists' Aren't Helping," *Daily Beast*, December 8, 2014, https://www.thedailybeast.com/techs-male-feminists-arent-helping.

179 Leigh Honeywell, "Bingo and Beyond," hypatia dot ca, September 23, 2015, https://hypatia.ca/2015/09/23/bingo-and-beyond/.

180 The 3% Movement, "Manbassador Bingo," 2015, https://image-store.slidesharecdn.com/846af5f5-84c2-4582-a02b-603d5a6349ae-original.jpeg.

CPSIA information can be obtained
at www.ICGtesting.com
Printed in the USA
LVHW010815080720
660059LV00009B/161/J

9 781732 723313